Improving
Schools
from Within

Roland S. Barth

with the editorial assistance of
Linda Sand Guest

Foreword by Theodore R. Sizer

Improving Schools from Within

*Teachers, Parents,
and Principals
Can Make
the Difference*

 Jossey-Bass Publishers

San Francisco • Oxford • 1990

IMPROVING SCHOOLS FROM WITHIN
Teachers, Parents, and Principals Can Make the Difference
by Roland S. Barth

Copyright © 1990 by: Jossey-Bass Inc., Publishers
350 Sansome Street
San Francisco, California 94104

&

Jossey-Bass Limited
Headington Hill Hall
Oxford OX3 0BW

Library of Congress Cataloging-in-Publication Data
Barth, Roland S.
    Improving schools from within : teachers, parents, and principals
can make the difference / Roland S. Barth, with the editorial
assistance of Linda Sand Guest.
        p.   cm. -- (Jossey-Bass education series)
    Includes bibliographical references (p. 181).
    ISBN 1-55542-215-2
    1. Public schools—United States.   2. School improvement programs—
United States.   3. College-school cooperation—United States.
    I. Title.   II. Series.
LA217.B38   1990
371'.01'0973--dc20   89-43460
                                                                    CIP

Manufactured in the United States of America

The paper in this book meets the guidelines for
permanence and durability of the Committee on
Production Guidelines for Book Longevity of the
Council on Library Resources.

Credits are on page 191.

JACKET DESIGN BY CHARLOTTE KAY GRAPHIC DESIGN

FIRST EDITION

Code 9027

The Jossey-Bass
Education Series

Contents

Foreword

Roland Barth trusts teachers. His remedies for our schools' ills arise from this trust in the energy, commitment, imagination, and potential of teachers and principals. Get the setting—the teachers' turf—right, he tells us, and the chances for good schooling will improve. By implication, he is saying more: Ignore the setting, or demean it, or assume that all settings are and should be alike, regardless of the teacher, and the schools will fail in their responsibility toward the students.

The secret to a good school setting is what Barth terms *collegiality*. At its heart, this social quality, which is more commonly associated with university faculty than with elementary school teachers, depends on respect of teachers and principals for themselves and for each other. People work hard in a place where colleagues listen well and take one another seriously (while not necessarily always agreeing) and where there is an expectation—even a demand—that everyone on the faculty can and must make a difference in the overall life of the school. Collegiality arises from the trust within a group; and trust is requisite when an institution of consequence—a school—depends on the honest expression of trust.

I know that many will scoff at these notions. Trust teachers? They aren't serious people. If they were, they wouldn't spend their time around overgrown babies or mewling adolescents. If they were smart enough to be trusted, they'd be businesspeople or lawyers. Why, let me tell you about a teacher my kid had. . . . Or, school is Serious Business and there is a lot that kids must know. The job of teachers is to get the material into the youngsters' heads, pure and simple. There are procedures for that. Instruct teachers to follow these procedures. An individual teacher's interests—much less Barth's romantic serendipity—have no place in an efficient knowledge factory. Why, let me tell you about my own schooling. . . . And you all know how successful I've been. . . .

There is some basis for such scoffing, but only some. Good teaching arises out of knowledge of particular youngsters and the ideas and skills that captivate them. Such wisdom is likely to arise only in people who know that they have the authority to act on it. Tell a teacher how to do everything and you deny that teacher the freedom to act on his or her wisdom. Able people—wise people—take jobs where they are entrusted with important tasks. Create a school without collegial trust and the authority to carry out improvements and you will create a third-rate school. Its faculty will be placeholders, not wise people.

Build a school on honest relationships, and the inept, confused, or slothful teacher will be exposed, unable to hide in her or his classroom. Create a climate of trust, and insecure teachers will develop confidence with the help of their colleagues. Put bluntly, a collegial school drives out incompetents and succors the temporarily weak. Strong teachers elicit the best from students and guide them in serious learning.

This book is not about children or schooling. It is, rather, about the adults who help children to learn. It is a realistic book. Sound and rich schools will emerge in America only when we trust, nurture, and respect teachers in a manner commensurate with the importance of the calling they have chosen. There are no short cuts to achieving educational excellence, no "teacher proof" techniques. Educational policy must start with high expectations for schools and ample trust in professionals. Policymakers must ponder Barth's important message.

January 1990   Theodore R. Sizer
                                                                 Brown University

Preface

As good as they may be, there is much about our public schools that needs improving—as any of us who have studied, been employed, or sent our children there can attest. This book is about improving schools. It is commonly held that public schools are incapable of reforming themselves. Many assume that if fundamental changes are made in American education, they will derive from the theories and practices prescribed by universities, federal and state governments, and the world of business. School improvement, if it comes at all, will come from without. Indeed, as I write, the city of Chelsea, Massachusetts, is conveying governance of its public schools into the waiting hands of Boston University—as if to confirm that the schools have tried and cannot do it; perhaps the university can do better.

Outside reformers usually wrestle with two questions: What do we want the schools to be like? And how do we get them to be that way? But the questions are shifting. Because outside prescriptions and interventions have led to disappointing results, because schoolpeople are asserting more responsibility for their own schools, and because promising models are being provided by industry, confidence is growing—by default as well as conviction—in increased governance and decision making at the school site. Many are coming to believe that those closest to students, and those likely to be most affected by the decisions, should make them. This guarded confidence in different forms of school-based management is posing a fundamentally different question with great implications for educators within the schools as well as outside them: Under what conditions that might be provided by those within schools, universities, state departments of education, and central offices will teachers, parents, principals, and students together create a promising vision for their schools and set out with the commitment to realize that vision? With this question we enter a period of fresh thinking about improving public schools.

Although much has been written about school reform in the past decade—national reports, studies, descriptions of findings—insufficient attention has been given to the important relationships among the adults within the school and to a consideration of how the abundant untapped energy, inventiveness, and idealism within the schoolhouse might be encouraged. *Improving Schools from Within* addresses this deficiency. One audience is university faculty and students, state department of education officials, and those in the school system's central office who are committed to helping schoolpeople reform their schools. Above all, though, this book is addressed to teachers, parents, and principals who want to, can, and must assume the major responsibility for getting their own schoolhouses in order.

The problem is that this is not an easy task. Already the fragile confidence in the capacity of those in schools to make decisions collaboratively and in the best interests of the school and of its students is being tested and shaken. Placing around a table three teachers, two parents, one principal, and a student who serve on a "school improvement team" does not make either for a team or for school improvement. Rather, it makes for three teachers, two parents, a principal, and a student sitting around a table.

As teacher, principal, and professor, I have always believed that schoolpeople can, working together, improve their schools—if only the conditions are right. For almost a decade, I have been teaching a year-long course at Harvard University, immodestly called Improving Schools. In the class, aspiring and practicing teachers, principals, superintendents, board members, librarians, social workers, curriculum specialists, and staff developers from around the country attempt to identify some of these conditions, impediments to their realization, and ways to work through the obstacles. Participants write frequent papers on topics such as "The conditions under which I learn best," "Leadership, for me, means. . . ," and "My vision of the kind of school in which I would like to work." They construct little cases around important, recurring school issues to which they have been a party—teacher evaluation, assignment of students to teachers, parent involvement, and professional development. Each student also serves as an intern in a school, attempting to bring to it a small measure of improvement.

During the last ten years, I have visited many schools and consulted with teachers, parents, and administrators. I have worked closely with the Principals' Center at Harvard University and with many of the hundred other centers, and I have written about school reform, attempting to clarify and articulate my own vision of "the kind of school I would like my children to attend."

Several hundred master's and doctoral degree candidates, a score of teaching fellows, and I have tried over the years, then, to collectively mine our school experiences and our thinking about improving schools for the gold they may contain. We have uncovered considerable gravel—but also some gold. We have developed a conviction not only that schools are capable of improving themselves but that, further, *only* changes emanating and sustained from within are likely to bring lasting improvement to our schools.

In this book, then, I take up the promising and perplexing issue of improving schools from within and consider the important relationships among the adults within the schoolhouse and the relationship of educators outside the school to those inside. This book is intended to further the fundamental purpose of schooling—learning, for everyone.

Overview of the Contents

In Chapter One I describe the widespread lack of confidence in public education and especially the crisis of self-

confidence and the primitive, depleting relationships among
the adults who serve in our nation's schools. In Chapter Two
I examine the relationship between teacher and principal—a
relationship that colors all other interactions and, thereby,
influences the quality of life for students and adults alike.

In the third chapter I consider collegiality, a valuable
and constructive form of adult interaction. I discuss why collegiality is so important to promoting learning and improving schools, and I offer some ideas for its cultivation. In the
fourth chapter I examine the logic behind many outside
attempts to improve schools and suggest why these efforts
rarely succeed. I introduce the concept of the school as a community of learners, where everyone is actively engaged in the
most important means of reform—learning.

In Chapters Five and Six I consider the importance of
teachers and principals as adult learners and examine some
of the sources of resistance they encounter to serious engagement in learning. I suggest how these obstacles may be overcome if some of the familiar and persistent elements of the
school culture are rearranged.

In Chapter Seven I describe my work with principals'
centers, which offer a promising means for extending the
place of the school principal from headmaster to head
learner—a role that is more conducive to promoting pupils'
and teachers' development. Chapter Eight deals with the
extraordinary benefits for teachers and principals of writing
about their important work in schools. I look at how writing
about practice can transform not only educators but their
students and schools as well. In Chapter Nine I address the
complicated relationship between universities and schools,
analyze some of the causes of tension between them, and offer
some ideas for a more fruitful collaboration. I consider how
universities might use their limited resources to help schoolpeople assume more responsibility for reforming their
schools.

I next look at leadership in schools (Chapter Ten), argu-
ing that everyone within a school—students, teachers, parents,
and administrators—is capable of leading and of becoming

an active member in "a community of leaders." I argue that the development of such a community is crucial to the very mission of a school.

In the final two chapters I consider the importance of vision in improving schools. I examine the possibility of gaining access to the rich personal visions that lie submerged within every teacher and principal. The last chapter conveys the central elements of my personal vision of a good school, which are reflected throughout the volume in anecdotes, examples, and incidents from my own school and university experience and in the words and experiences of many other school practitioners.

Acknowledgments

Improving Schools from Within has been inspired by many teachers, parents, and principals, and I am indebted to them for their hard-won insights. I have attempted here to convey to a wider audience the considered and considerable, yet often unrecognized, craft knowledge of these many school-people, in the hope that others will also take the lead in improving their schools. Improving schools from within is, I believe, an important, a timely, and above all a hopeful journey.

Finally, I want to thank Lesley Iura, Kent D. Peterson, Marilyn Posner, and Richard Streedain for their helpful comments on the manuscript. And I thank Linda Sand Guest for her assistance in editing, especially during the early stages. I want to express my indebtedness to Lucianne B. Carmichael for helping me clarify my vision. Thanks go, too, to Vanessa Barth for her sustained magic on the word processor. And to Beth Barth for seeing me through.

Cambridge, Massachusetts   Roland S. Barth
January 1990

To the memory of my father,
Joseph N. Barth,
who taught me
more than I know

The Author

Roland S. Barth is senior lecturer on education at Harvard University. He received his A.B. degree (1959) from Princeton University in psychology and his Ed.M. (1962) and Ed.D. (1970) degrees from the Harvard Graduate School of Education, in elementary education, and curriculum and supervision, respectively. He served as a public school teacher and principal for fifteen years in Massachusetts, Connecticut, and California and as an assistant to deans at Princeton and Harvard.

From 1979 to 1980 Barth was director of the Study on the Harvard Graduate School of Education and Schools. He was the founding director of the Principals' Center at Harvard and more recently has been the project director of the National Network of Principals' Centers. He teaches at Harvard in the fields of school leadership and school improvement. Barth served as facilitator for the Danforth Foundation's Program for Professors of School Administration and was a member of the National Commission on Excellence in Educational Administration. In 1977 he was the recipient of a Guggenheim Fellowship, and in 1986 he was an academic visitor at the Department of Educational studies, Oxford University. He is the author of many articles and of two other books: *Open Education and the American School* (1972) and *Run School Run* (1980).

Improving
Schools
from Within

Introduction

A tennis shoe in a laundry dryer. Probably no image captures so fully for me the life of an adult working in an elementary, middle, or senior high school. For educators schoolwork much of the time is turbulent, heated, confused, disoriented, congested, and full of recurring bumps.

What does it feel like after fifteen years to suddenly emerge from the laundry dryer? Several years ago I received a grant to write a book about life in a school. I suddenly found myself, feet on the ground, upright, out in the cool dry air of daylight. It felt very strange, and very welcome. I tried to make some sense out of this unfamiliar moment by writing a letter to fellow principals who were in school when I was out:

Dear Friends,

Here I sit—at a typewriter before a wood stove in a nineteenth-century farmhouse, secluded in the Village of Head Tide, in the town of Alna, in the County of Lincoln, a third of the way "down" the coast of Maine, near nothing and nobody in particular, save trees, rocks, fields, and my wife and two daughters. There you sit— 180 miles away in twenty-two different schools spread over the thirteen villages of Newton, facing each day the delights and despairs so familiar to public school administrators in these times.

I can't help reflecting on the juxtaposition of what I was doing a year ago (and what you are doing today) with what I am doing now. It first became apparent this

1

year was to be different for me from the past nine I have spent as a school principal when, toward the end of August, I began to read the daily paper.

Since school let out in June, I had found no particular need to know what was going on over the rest of the planet. On the contrary, my body and head both sought to minimize external stimulation as much as possible. But partly because it was getting colder and we needed newspaper to kindle the morning fire, partly because I was interested to see if the Red Sox were still in the pennant race, and partly because I was beginning to wonder if there was life outside Head Tide, I subscribed to the *Boston Globe*. What struck me most was not the world situation or the standings in the American League East, but the advertisements. "Back-to-school sales" at Sears, Woolworth's, and King's were the news—new clothes, book bags, lunch boxes, and notebooks.

It suddenly became clear to me that for years and years, these ads have served as my early warning system—as a second grader, a high school student, a teacher, and then as a school principal. The back-to-school sales, accompanied by occasional falling leaves and crisp northwest gusts, annually produced in my gut a feeling that can only be described as panic. These were the end-of-August feelings that, as a kid, propelled me to drive the nocturnal back roads setting off cherry bombs and two-inchers in RFD mailboxes, and that later led to sober, solitary walks by the river, overwhelmed with the contemplation and consternation of a condemned inmate scheduled for sunrise execution.

In more recent years, since we've had the farm, my response to back-to-school announcements has changed. I have here an old 1953 Ford tractor that, despite its years, tows behind it a big, six-foot rotary mower with tough, sharp steel blades. At 1,600 RPM it can obliterate almost anything it comes near—usually brush, hay, and occasional woodchuck mounds and ground hornets' nests. My friend over in Whitefield says, "You can always tell when it's time for Roland to go back to school because the tractor and mower leave the fields, and Roland heads into the woods to open up woodroads, driving at full throttle over stumps, rocks, and pine trees with a clatter that can be heard over on the West Alna road."

I used to chuckle about the irony of this change in my driving habits just as the perennial bumper stickers began to announce, "School's Open, Drive Carefully." I even thought about putting one of those stickers on the side of the tractor to help me come to grips with the relationship between schools and tractors. To be truthful, I've had little success over the years in dealing with the end of summer and the beginning of school.

For a decade, the overriding reality had been, "You are about to embark on ten months of uninterrupted work, orchestrating the disparate and desperate needs of 400 students, twice as many parents, 30 teachers, legions of central office people, and 9 school board persons." I used to tell myself, "Remember, you don't have to get through the whole year without a breather. Just make it to Columbus Day." But respites like Thanksgiving, Christmas, and spring vacation, while offering some consolation, did not and could not prevent conscious and unconscious preoccupation with the nagging discomfort, fear, and anger that accompany setting limits on adults and children, and that precede and follow known violation of what others want, expect, and demand. Indeed, in recent years, I've found it all but impossible to shake these lingering worries during a two-month summer vacation, let alone during shorter holidays.

I can be in the middle of a hot hay field in July when suddenly I'm wondering if those two teachers across the hall from one another are going to get along this year—and what I'm going to do if they don't. Or I can be sailing out on Muscongus Bay between Eastern Egg Rock and Franklin Light when I begin to think about redistricting the sixth graders to a new junior high school next year—the one where parents fought to have their children remain six years ago when the previous districting took place. Or I can be out picking blueberries in August when I'm reminded of the PTA meeting last winter when parents demanded our complete and uniform faculty compliance with the citywide English curriculum guidelines.

It's clear that working in a school—while technically a ten-month job with some evenings and weekends off—is, as you and I know, a full-time occupation, one that can never be completely abandoned, escaped, or shaken. It follows us like a silent shadow in the berry patch, on the bay, or into the middle of the night.

I think I would live more at peace with that shadow if the image it conveyed from time to time silhouetted the joys and satisfactions that are also a large part of my experience as a principal. But somehow, over the years, the ratio of high-anxiety, disturbing recollections to peaceful, satisfying ones has gotten way out of line. I remember telling the staff at a meeting last spring that the ratio of problems to solutions had been at about five to one—and holding. That was the same day I had my annual physical examination and was warned that my blood pressure was approaching dangerous limits. The constant worries of teachers and principals exact all sorts of tolls, revealed through all sorts of symptoms.

Well, as I read the back-to-school notices last month, it became evident to me that the annual panic and despair, as predictable each year as the equinox or solstice, were largely gone. I can't begin to describe how relieved I felt. In their place are new worries and new anxieties, but of a totally different sort. Is the house sufficiently insulated for winter? Will I be able to lay in six or eight cords of hardwood before snowfall? Will the new wood furnace heat up the basement so much that the root vegetables, apples, and squash stored there will spoil?

I'm finding these concerns, and the tasks associated with them, somehow less worrisome and more
satisfying than those I face as a principal. Take the
wood, for instance. Yesterday I went out with tractor,
trailer, and chain saw and spent the day felling, cutting,
and stacking about a cord of red oak. At dinnertime I
felt both tired and satisfied; tired by physical exertion in
the absence of emotional stress, and satisfied because
there was nearly a cord of wood piled alongside the cellar
door where that morning there was none.

Contrast the quality of that tiredness with the tiredness I recall after a day in the principal's office—being
tired from emotional stress without physical exertion.
Contrast the certainty of a woodpile with the uncertainty
of the outcome of a day in the office. In the morning, I
knew there were five parents coming to see me about
their children's class assignments for the following year.
At 5:00 P.M., there were still five parents unhappy about
their children's teachers for next year—or were they?
What was accomplished? The placement decisions would
stick—or would they? The parents wouldn't persist—or
would they? What changes, progress, or improvements
in the world could be attributed to my day's work? The
only clear evidence that I had even done a day's work
seemed to be the personal and interpersonal bruises.
Uncertainties were many and resolutions few.

I'm reminded of what Junior Burns, the farmer
down at the foot of the hill, said a few days ago. Junior
cuts our fields and feeds the hay to his dairy cows. In
return he gives me all the manure I want for my gardens
and apple trees. On a drizzling day, I was loading the
spreader and slipping around a bit, when Junior came
out of the barn after milking. He leaned against the barn
door, knocked his pipe against the stone step, paused,
and said, "Roland, no matter what you do, that's good
preparation for it!"

From a distance of several months and several
miles, I find myself recalling peculiar things about my

life as a principal. Take my office, for example. I recall the two windows, both facing north. It has occurred to me several times this fall, as I sit waiting for words and ideas to put themselves together, that from 7:00 or 8:00 A.M. to 4:00 or 5:00 P.M., 190 days a year for six years, I never saw or felt the sunshine—that my office is a place designed for or are capable of sustaining. But like the windows without sunlight, but both are covered on the outside by a heavy mesh of iron bars. The other windows on the first floor have no such protection. Why the principal's office? Is it to keep the rocks out, or to keep the principal in, I wonder.

Take the doors in the office. There are three. I say that one is for parents, one for children, and one for teachers. But now that I think of it, it's strange for such a small room to have three different doors, and even more peculiar that all of them, despite my declaration that "my door is always open," remain closed for the greater part of each day. I tell myself that it is because of the seriousness and confidentiality of the business being discussed inside. Is that really the reason, or would I prefer no doors at all?

Take my desk. I moved it against a wall so that it would not come between me and the person with whom I was talking. But every time I pull out the top drawer, I am confronted with an assortment of confiscated knives— a peculiar inventory, to be sure. What does it signify? Take the bottom right-hand drawer. Last spring I kept parents' letters requesting specific placements for their children in that drawer, right next to two salt shakers and a bottle of aspirin. Interesting. Take the left middle drawer, which, despite its cluttered neighbors, always remained empty. It reminds me of the time I sent one of you a note saying, "This memo needs no reply, phone call, or action. It raises no problems nor expects any solutions. Just wanted to say hi!" What does it all mean?

I'm sure each of you has similar peculiarities in your own school world. It occurs to me now that these things become less and less peculiar the more we live with them. Someone has said a fish would be the last to discover water. So, too, only when we stand back, as I am now doing, are some of the obvious absurdities of our lives in a school environment revealed. That's what I find happening this year.

Remember the story of the farmer boy whose cow gave birth to a little calf? Every day the boy would carry the calf up the mountain to the pasture and return with it in the evening. At first the little animal weighed only fifty pounds, but every day the calf gained a pound or two—an inconsequential amount, of course, and an increment the boy could easily bear. As the calf grew into a cow, the boy continued to carry it up the mountain, despite its weight of 1,500 pounds. It was an extraordinary load, but because the boy had been carrying the calf from its infancy, and because each daily increment was small, it was possible for him to carry an animal ten times his own weight up a mountain.

I think there is a message here for those of us who work in schools. Over the years, we have assumed small, discrete additions to our responsibilities: for the safe passage of children from their homes to school; for ensuring that the sidewalks are plowed of snow; for maintaining the physical condition of the building. We have taken on responsibility for children's achievement of minimal standards at each grade level; responsibility for children with special needs, for the gifted, and for those who are neither; and responsibility for administering tests, trying to ensure that as many children as possible score above average, and reporting the scores to the public.

Not one of those responsibilities is backbreaking in itself, but collectively they present an enormous burden that is perhaps many times greater than we were designed for or are capable of sustaining. But like the locomotive in "The Little Engine That Could," we keep trying and puffing, "I think I can, I think I can."

Remember our end-of-year banquet last June when we acknowledged no fewer than six of our twenty-two colleagues who were leaving? There were many reasons, of course, for that unusual turnover—retirements, leaves, sabbaticals, school closings—but I can't help wondering now if beneath all of those reasons is a common factor: that only up to a point can we, will we, continue to carry the cow up the mountain. Beyond that point, the load becomes an inhuman burden to bear. Beyond that point, we've had enough. It is a disturbing insight, one I have come to confront only now, at this point in my year's leave of absence. And as others might ask of the farmer boy because he was not asking it of himself, I find myself asking, Why have I been carrying the cow up and down the mountain every day? Do I have any choice? Is it possible for the cow to walk up the mountain? Is it necessary for the cow to go up the mountain at all?

Without the distance from school that I enjoy this year, these would be difficult questions to ask. From my present vantage point, they have become difficult—and compelling—questions to answer.

I hope you have a good year. Let's keep in touch.

Cheers,
Roland

I suspect that any adult who was given the opportunity to step out of the laundry dryer to reflect on work in a school might compose a version of this letter, a disturbing mixture of tedium and hopefulness. It is difficult to be a student in school, day after day, class after class, homework assignment after homework assignment. And it may be even tougher to be a teacher or a parent or a principal.

When I wrote the letter I was on leave of absence, fully intending to return. I did not. Rather, I accepted a temporary position at Harvard that has now extended well beyond a decade. As I continue to contemplate this dramatic turning point in my life, I often think I would not have left my career in schools if . . . I would have gone back if . . . I will go back when . . . Or, when I return I will . . . This way I will not be consumed by the experience, and more of my energy will become available to help students and other adults improve the school.

In the pages that follow I attempt to fill in these blanks, for myself and possibly for others who continue to courageously labor in our nation's schools. I want to make explicit just what I have found missing in the school culture for adults, and, more important, what life in school for grownups might and can become.

Central to my conception of a good school and a healthy workplace is community. In particular, I would want to return to work in a school that could be described as a *community of learners,* a place where students and adults alike are engaged as active learners in matters of special importance to them and where everyone is thereby encouraging everyone else's learning. And I would readily work in a school that could be described as a *community of leaders,* where students, teachers, parents, and administrators share the opportunities and responsibilities for making decisions that affect all the occupants of the schoolhouse.

The concepts of school as a community of learners and leaders will recur in these pages as organizing principles for what a school might become. Other elements of a compelling school for adults support these two. I would welcome the chance to work in a school characterized by a high level of collegiality, a place teeming with frequent, helpful personal and professional interactions. I would become excited about life in a school where a climate of risk taking is deliberately fostered and where a safety net protects those who may risk and stumble. I would like to go each day to a school to be with other adults who genuinely wanted to be there, who really chose to be there because of the importance of their work to others and to themselves. I would not want to leave a school characterized by a profound respect for and encouragement of diversity, where important differences among children and adults were celebrated rather than seen as problems to remedy. For 190 days each year, I would like to attend an institution that accorded a special place to philosophers who constantly examine and question and frequently replace embedded practices by asking "why" questions. And I could even reside for a while in a laundry dryer if accompanied by a great deal of humor that helps bond the community by assisting everyone through tough moments. I'd like to work in a school that constantly takes note of the stress and anxiety level on the one hand, and standards on the other, all the while searching for the optimal relationship of low anxiety and high standards.

These are the important themes that have occupied my discussions with school practitioners and my thinking about school improvement these past years. And these are the themes that will occupy us here. For me, writing these pages has been at once a personal, professional, and collective journey to find meaning in the hurly-burly world of schools, to move from disorientation toward orientation, and to consider the school that no one would want to leave and to which everyone would want to recommit. I hope that what follows may encourage others to juxtapose what is with what might be, and more important, to begin to transfer the school that is into the school we would like it to be.

ONE

A Crisis of Confidence

A medieval curse, uttered as a final expression of pique and condemnation, resounds, "May you have to teach other people's children." Many contemporary educators are discovering its meaning. Teaching other people's children has become an extraordinarily difficult occupation, made no easier by "other people" who hold little confidence in what educators do and pare away the resources with which they are expected to do it. Public educators—superintendents, teachers, principals—have never enjoyed highly revered positions in American society. Yet in difficult times they have been fueled by a sense of their own mission and public recognition of the social usefulness of their work. But a decade of decline in test scores, enrollments, resources, and public confidence now makes it clear that the public lacks commitment to public education in general, and confidence in its educators in particular. The cumulative effect of rejected bond issues, placement of children in private schools, school closings, and governmental devaluation of education is an unmistakable message. What public educators are doing is not only not good, it is not worthwhile.

We have heard parts of this message before. But I now see too many educators believing it. As a result, schools face not only a crisis of public confidence but, more dangerous, a crisis of self-confidence. Not only can we no longer expect that citizens without school-age children will support education, we can no longer assume that people *with* school-age children will offer up their progeny and patronage. Even

11

worse, we can no longer take for granted that those who staff our public schools believe that they are engaged in a vital cause.

A Harvard graduate student who observed at a respected suburban high school reported that the faculty feels:

A sense of discontent and malaise. They feel unappreciated, overworked, not respected as professionals, undersupported, undervalued, and unrewarded.

A low sense of trust toward the administration, the public, and even among themselves. They feel they are not trusted by their superiors or the public.

Separated from one another—compartmentalized. They express a sense of competition among departments for resources, for students, and for jobs as well.

Helpless and trapped in their jobs, powerless to effect change. They see the causes of the situation as beyond their control. They do not feel in charge of their work lives.

A sense of frustration at the "nonteaching" demands placed upon them. They feel it is increasingly difficult to be effective as teachers and to fulfill the other requirements of the job.

Schools these days are staffed more and more with veteran, tenured personnel who have little horizontal or vertical mobility. For most there is little to do this September except what they did last September—more of the same. Same books, same room, same colleagues, same curriculum. Only pupils are different from one year to the next. But the burden for the professional health of adults in schools should not rest with students.

Add to the highly routinized work of schoolpeople the expectation to do more with less. More pupils per class, more evidence of pupil achievement, and more energy in a climate of decline in the number of students, in test scores, in the number of jobs, in resources, in morale, and in public confidence. Many teachers would probably agree with what one fourth-grade teacher told me recently: "Excellence is no longer an appropriate goal toward which I aspire. Now I'm satisfied if I can do it at all, let alone well."

The message is pretty clear: Teachers are encountering times probably more difficult than at any period in American history. The social value of their work, which has fueled them through past difficulties, is no longer able to provide sufficient compensation and professional invigoration. One question facing many schoolpeople is, "Will there be a job for me next year?" But an even more compelling question has become, "Will I want it if there is one for me?"

The erosion of the inch-by-inch gains by mile-by-mile losses is too much for too many. Expecting more for less is not a formula that attracts and retains talent. I'm afraid many would agree with one principal who told me, "I'd leave tomorrow if I could afford it. I've paid my dues in public service with little recognition over the years. Now it's time for myself." And a 1989 national survey of teachers conducted by the National Education Association revealed that less than half of all teachers responding would want their sons or daughters to enter the teaching profession (Elam, 1989, p. 791).

What we educators do out of school reveals an equal degree of malaise. I recall three end-of-the-year parties held in the Boston area. The first party honored a superintendent who had resigned after more than a dozen years of distinguished service. Following months of torment within the school community, exacerbated by declining public confidence, he was leaving to take a position in a university. At the conclusion of his going-away party, I'm told, a huge cake was brought out. Handsomely crafted in the icing loomed the unmistakable profile of a sinking ship.

The second party recognized an outstanding teacher whose nine years of dedicated work were insufficient to prevent her from being laid off because of decreased enrollment. I attended this event expecting to find a coterie of friends and colleagues attesting to her professional capability and lamenting her dismissal. Instead, I discovered the major theme of the banter and conversation among her colleagues was one of anger, resentment, and envy that *they* were not being "released." Or, as I have heard teachers say, "The three best reasons for teaching are June, July, and August." Public schools all too often seem every bit as "compulsory" for teachers as for their students.

The third party was attended by some of the most able school principals in the Boston area. Over in a corner of the room someone asked a stranger to the group—the husband of one of the principals—what he did for a living. He answered that he was a personnel recruiter for a hi-tech company in Boston. The conversation in the entire room abruptly ceased as everyone looked with renewed interest at this man. E. F. Hutton could have done no better.

Each of these not-very-festive, out-of-school events illustrates the same sobering in-school message: The best and the brightest are leaving public education. And a huge number of the educators who remain will serve their time only until something more lucrative, socially valued, personally fulfilling, and less consuming comes along.

What a public school system can deliver to children when many of its employees are in a holding pattern is something to worry about. Fortunately, the crisis in teaching—attracting capable persons into the profession, preparing them in the classroom, retaining them, and supporting them in their important work—has become an issue of national importance, as the work of the Carnegie Forum on Education and the Economy (1986) and the Holmes Group (1986), for example, attests. It remains to determine under what conditions teaching can become less of a job and more of a profession.

Varied solutions to the problems of public education parade before us. Government solutions call for more stringent standards for graduation from high school, higher standards for teacher certification, and more rigid enforcement of discipline codes. Others propose improving all teachers' salaries; compensating the best teachers through merit pay; constructing career ladders that will pay those who assume more responsibility; supporting the training of top students so they will choose to enter teaching; and making teacher evaluation more rigorous. Although these proposals promise much, they tend to be outside-of-school remedies to inside-of-school problems. Rarely do they work their way into the fabric of the school or into educators' lives, and even more rarely into classrooms. Therefore, they offer only modest hope of influencing the basic culture of the schools. And it is in the ethos of the workplace where the problems reside and where, I believe, the most promising solutions reside as well. The moment of truth for the educator comes when the alarm rings at 6:30 A.M. How does the teacher respond? Higher salaries, career ladders, and certification requirements will have little impact on the reaction of the waking teacher.

The reasons many proposed solutions to the woes of public schools seldom influence the culture of our schools are complex and permeate the entire educational community. For me, the issue revolves around the nature of adults' personal and professional relationships within schools. The success of a school, I believe, depends above all on the quality of interactions between teacher and teacher, and teacher and administrator. These contacts take many forms.

Parallel Play

There is a wonderful term from nursery school parlance: *parallel play*. Two four-year-olds are busily engaged in opposite corners of a sandbox. Jimmy has a shovel and a bucket; Susan is playing with a rake and a hoe. At no time does Jimmy use Susan's rake or hoe nor does Susan borrow Jimmy's bucket or shovel, let alone do they build a sand castle together. They may inadvertently throw sand in each other's face from time to time, but seldom do they interact. Although in close proximity for long periods of time and having much to offer one another, each works and plays pretty much in isolation.

Parallel play, thought to be a developmental stage through which three- and four-year-olds pass, holds remarkably well as a characterization of adult relationships in schools—elementary schools, middle schools, high schools, and universities. Teachers develop subtle strategies for trying to influence the domain of others but seldom venture there or relate substantively when they do. A taboo prevents one teacher from observing another teacher who is engaged in the act of teaching. Mutual visibility is not a hallmark of the teaching profession. Rather, a third-grade teacher on one side of the hall carefully circumvents the teaching space of the third-grade teacher on the other side of the hall.

In many schools the taboo extends well beyond the classroom, as an almost unbelievable field note of a graduate student suggests: "The teachers' lunchroom contains fifteen large tables. When I visited during one lunch period each table was occupied by a single, silent, teacher." And one principal in a system seldom visits the school of another. I remember once suggesting to the principals in Newton that more of us had visited schools in Great Britain than in our own system. A quick poll supported this observation. University professors, too, have been described as "a group of isolated individuals connected by a common heating system and parking lot." We all seem to have an implied contract: Don't intrude on me as I do my work and I won't bother you as you try to do yours.

In schools, like sandboxes, the benefit of parallel play is isolation from others who might take our time, challenge our practice, steal our ideas, or have us do things differently. The price of parallel play is, of course, that we ward off those who might help us to do things better and with whom together we might do grander things than either could do alone. And the price is isolation from other adults.

But, of course, all adult relationships in schools are not independent.

Adversarial Relationships

Recently, a school principal observed: "You know, we educators have drawn our wagons into a circle and trained our guns—on each other." When adults in school do interact, when we leave our parallel play, all too often we attack one another. There's no dearth of enemies outside of education, of course, but somehow we manage to create opponents under our own roofs. In order for me to win, you must lose. One teacher badmouths another to gain parents' support. A principal evaluates a teacher by obliterating the teacher. One parent gains special services for a needy child, but in order to provide those services the teacher must take from children of other parents. And so it goes. It may be that the depleting adversarial relationships among adults in school are what make parallel play such a welcome, common alternative.

Competitive Relationships

A third form of adult relationships within schools is competition. A wish for all of us in school is to succeed, perhaps, and for our school to be better than others, but most of all for *me* to excel. This may mean neither avoidance nor throwing sand. Typically, it means withholding. I find that most schoolpeople carry around with them extraordinary insights about their important work—garnered from years of rich experience—about discipline, parent involvement, budgeting, child development, leadership, and curriculum. These hard-won insights are certainly of as much value to other practitioners as elegant research studies and national reports. But adults in school display an extraordinary reluctance to make these insights available to others who are competitors for scarce resources and recognition—that is, almost everyone else. Nor does anyone want to be considered pretentious by professing this knowledge. Woe to the teacher who stands up in a faculty meeting and offers: "I have a great idea about grouping children in mathematics. I want to share it with all of you." Consequently, all the talk each day among teachers and parents and administrators notwithstanding, a taboo prevails in many schools against one practitioner sharing craft knowledge with another.

One school I visited had a sign boldly written on the door of the teachers' lounge: "No students allowed in the teachers' room." When asked about that, a teacher replied: "That's the *written* rule; the *unwritten* rule is: "No talking about teaching in the teachers' room."

How can a profession survive, let alone flourish, when its members are cut off from each other and from the rich knowledge base upon which success and excellence depend? Not very well. Professional isolation stifles professional growth. There can be no community of learners when there is no community and when there are no learners.

What is giving rise in our schools to the debilitating parallel play, to adversarial and competitive relationships, and to professional isolation? I believe that these problems are rooted in the relationship between teacher and principal, to which I now turn.

TWO

Adversaries Within
the Schoolhouse

There are many important relationships within a school: child-child, teacher-teacher, child-teacher, parent-teacher, parent-principal, parent-parent. I am convinced that none of these relationships has greater effect on the quality of life under the roof of the schoolhouse than the relationship between teacher and principal. I have found no characteristic of a good school more pervasive than a healthy teacher-principal relationship—and no characteristic of a troubled school more common than a troubled, embattled administrator-teacher relationship.

My experience suggests that as it goes between teacher and principal so shall it go in the other relationships. If the teacher-principal relationship can be characterized as helpful, supportive, trusting, revealing of craft knowledge, so too will others. To the extent that teacher-principal interactions are suspicious, guarded, distant, adversarial, acrimonious, or judgmental, we are likely to see these traits pervade the school. The relationship between teacher and principal seems to have an extraordinary amplifying effect. It models what *all* relationships will be.

Problems in Teacher-Principal Relationships

Unfortunately, things between teachers and principals these days have become increasingly strained with growing emphasis on teacher empowerment, pupil minimum compe-

19

tency, collective bargaining, declines in student population, reduction in teacher force, increased litigation, and above all "accountability."

The pathology of the principal-teacher relationship in many schools is symbolized by what one teacher termed "the parking lot syndrome." As a new principal, I prepared carefully for my first faculty meeting. I arranged chairs in circles, and encouraged several teachers to contribute. Yet, during the meeting I found I did most of the talking while teachers sat quietly by. A few minutes after the meeting, I looked out my office window at the school parking lot and realized where the *real* faculty meeting was taking place. Little clusters of teachers were abuzz, expressing their ideas about all the subjects on the agenda.

In a conversation among some teachers and principals in New York State, one secondary school teacher observed: "In my career I have taught 17,000 classes." Wow! When the shock of that statement had settled, the speaker continued. "And during those 17,000 classes there has been another adult in my room on *eight* occasions." 8/17,000—a decidedly improper fraction. Finally the teacher concluded, "And each of the visitors was a principal there to evaluate my work."

These two vignettes reveal what most schoolpeople know too well: In faculty meetings, principals talk; in parking lots and classrooms, teachers talk. But seldom do teachers and principals talk openly together about their important work.

Most principals I know leave the classroom for the principal's office propelled by the idealism of improving a school, as well as expecting to enhance their professional and personal standing in some way. These teachers become administrators because they experienced years of frustration, fatigue, uncertainty, and intermittent satisfaction all too familiar to teachers. Fueled by the conviction that they can do more for teachers and can run the school better than their predecessor, beginning principals arrive at their desks sympathetic to teachers, committed to providing support and helping make their impossible job more possible. In short, most new principals begin as teacher colleagues and advocates. "I'm one of you. I'm your friend."

Then something happens. In only a few months principals are transformed—not by choice, design, or wish—from teacher advocates to teacher adversaries. Something within the peculiar, cruel culture of schools and school systems converts good intentions into bad relationships and changes colleagues into superordinates and subordinates. Something in the alchemy of schools contorts friends who would help teachers into administrators who require more and tolerate less. The teacher who becomes principal emerges from the chrysalis a different species—all too often part of teachers' problems rather than their solutions.

Recently I talked with a teacher whose long-time, trusted teaching partner had just become principal of her school. The teacher related that the friend-principal had come into the teacher's classroom the other day to observe. Surprisingly, the teacher felt "scared to death," and was astonished at what a change in professional titles had suddenly done to a long-standing friendship. Trust had given way to suspicion, openness had been replaced by guardedness, and pleasure by pain. I find that this disturbing anecdote attests to the mysterious powers at work within our schools. What accompanies the metamorphosis from teacher into principal is disheartening not only for teachers, but for administrators as well.

To be sure, we can all point to teacher-principal relationships that are relaxed, close, helpful, trusting, and stable. But we can't point to many—and there appear to be fewer and fewer. What happens? What's going on? In schools, this is both a highly personal question and one with far-reaching professional implications. As teachers are expected to do more and more with less and less, the principal has become an even more critical figure, capable of both creating and reducing teachers' problems.

I have been away from schools for several years now. But this distance is not so great that as every March and April roll around I forget the perennial issues that come between teacher and principal at this time of year and that can poison their relationship. I have long felt that how it goes in a school in the spring is a reliable indicator not only of the year's success, but of the school's success as well.

For a few teachers, springtime is depressing. Things have grown thin between teacher and children. They have exhausted their ideas and themselves, done what they could for their students and found it less than adequate, and now count the days until the end of the year. They fill up the balance with parties, field trips, worksheets, and tests. For many others, March and April mark the *middle* of the year. They wonder how they will ever be able to finish all the things they want to do with their classes by June. They have completed half of their objectives, and the calendar attests that three-fourths of the year is over. And, above all, spring is the time of year when the quality of the adult relationships within a school that contribute so much to its character and success become challenged and strained. It is a time when schoolpeople live simultaneously in the past, dwelling on what kind of a year it has been; in the present, worrying whether they can possibly manage; and in the future, preoccupied with what's going to happen next year. In schools, spring can be the best of times and the worst of times.

Let me recall some of the springtime issues that, for many years, dominated my life as a teacher and a principal— issues of the sort that contribute a good deal to the tension between teacher and principal: the year-end teacher evaluations of pupils; the principal's evaluation of teachers; each teacher's place in next year's school organization; and the assignment of children to teachers' classes for next year.

Just the mention of these tasks immediately calls up several anxiety-laden associations for teachers and principals. Yet seldom do teachers and principals worry together, and seldom are teachers and principals worrying about the same thing when they worry about these same issues. This worry in isolation heavily colors the teacher-principal relationship. Let me try to recall some typical questions that are seldom verbalized but often asked by teachers and principals.

Pupil Evaluation: Teacher. "In previous reports and conferences I have told the parents all I know about their children's strengths and weaknesses, improvements and lack of improvements. Things haven't changed much since January. What more can I say now? What more *is* there to say? I wish I could appraise children's work the way I want and not be compelled to use the official form. How can I possibly summon the time and energy to pull together my ideas about twenty-eight children, write the reports, each of which must be unique for each child, and then schedule and hold another round of conferences? How shall I write a progress report on Robert, Michael, and Abby, who have not made much progress this year, have not tested well, and have not gained much from my program—without the principal blaming me for their failure?"

Pupil Evaluation: Principal. "What combination of carrots and sticks can I employ this time to motivate teachers to approach their end-of-year evaluations with enthusiasm, imagination, and commitment when most are worn down, if not worn out, capable of little enthusiasm, imagination, and commitment for a task they have done so often before? How can I get teachers to evaluate children using a uniform format so it looks like we know what we're doing in this school? How can I assure and reassure parents that their children are all doing 'above average' work when half of the children are doing 'below average' work? Why are so many children testing poorly and making little progress in Ms. Green's and Mr. Jones's rooms? What shall I do about these teachers? What's going to happen when the local newspaper publishes our test scores and they don't measure up to those of other schools?"

Principal's Evaluation of Teachers—Principal's Viewpoint. "How can I get through another round of these evaluations? I've already said all there is to say. How can I make some substantive suggestions for improvement without alarming or antagonizing the staff? How can my teacher evaluations be kind, gentle, supportive, and general enough to maintain

trust and confidence with teachers, while at the same time
sufficiently hard nosed, incisive, and specific to bring some
change and convince the director of personnel, superintendent,
and school board that I am a rigorous supervisor? When am I
ever going to find the time to sit in on enough classes and
hold the pre- and post-conferences, so that when I make observations or suggestions for improvement—or the recommendation not to reappoint—I will have sufficient data to withstand
a teacher's *'I* don't think my class is too noisy! On what basis
do you make that accusation?' I know some teachers will share
everything I say with friends on the staff and then what will I
do? This whole business is so damned unpleasant. I'm not
sure I can go through it again."

*Principal's Evaluation of Teachers—A Teacher's View-
point.* "I wonder what the principal's going to find fault
with this time? How can I protect myself? How can I put on
a good show, and be sure the kids will cooperate when the
principal comes in? I think I will be recommended for reappointment. I always have been before. But then, with declining enrollment things are different. I just might not be. Come
to think of it, the principal has been a bit evasive lately. How
can someone come in here and expect to see a perfect lesson
each time? The principal doesn't know these kids. I wish
someone else would try to teach this class—just once—and let
me sit at the back of the room and take notes! How can I
keep pretending to welcome the principal in 'anytime' when
I resent being checked up on all the time? This whole business is so damned unpleasant. I'm not sure I can go through
it again."

*The Teacher's Place in the School Organization from a
Teacher's Perspective.* "I wish I could take a year off and do
something really different next year. Travel, go back to school,
or just rest. If I stay, I want to teach fourth grade in this room
next year. Otherwise, I'll have to spend all summer fixing up
a new room and preparing a new program. But there won't
be enough students for three fourth grades. One of us will

have to make a move—or take a combination third-fourth class. It won't be me. I won't do it. I wonder what else the principal might have in mind?"

Be ...

The Teacher's Place in the School Organization from the Principal's Perspective. "I wish some teacher would retire or transfer so I didn't have to reassign a teacher who does not want to be reassigned. But it seems like more children are leaving the school and more teachers are staying. Which of the fourth-grade teachers will I move? I think Mr. Simmons would give me the least grief. But is that a good enough reason to choose him? What will the other teachers, the parents, and the central office say? What if he files a grievance or goes to the parents or the school board? What if the staff rallies behind him? How can I make the class sizes equitable when there are forty children in third grade and fifty-six in fourth? Parents and teachers won't buy a discrepancy between twenty and twenty-eight students in a class. Maybe a combined class. One third, two fourths, and a third–fourth. That's a monster. What teacher would touch it? Would enough parents accept placement of their children in a third–fourth? How could I sell it to parents with a reluctant teacher teaching it? I wonder which would cause fewer problems, big difference in class sizes or introducing a third–fourth? Why does it always boil down to the best of two bad alternatives?"

Placement of Children: A Teacher's Concerns. "How can I make sure all of my kids will go into Ms. Lopez's or Ms. Ryan's rooms, but not into Mr. Lemon's? How can I prevent a bunch of disturbed, disturbing kids from being assigned to me next year? What if only a few teachers or parents want their kids in my class next year?"

Placement of Children: Principal's Concerns. "How can I ever balance the classes with girls and boys, leaders and followers, and fast and slow, when teachers and parents—and the kids themselves—all have such strong teacher preferences? I hope somehow supply and demand will balance out this year. What will I do about Johnny? His teacher, the psychologist, and I all think he should go into Ms. Ryan's class, but his parents will have none of it. How am I ever going to fill Mr. Lemon's class? No one wants children in there. How can I sell that class when I wouldn't want one of my own children there? What am I going to do about Mr. Lemon?"

Pupil evaluation, teacher evaluation, staff organization, and placement of children are examples of springtime school regularities for both teacher and principal. But an examination of the all too typical and painful concerns that accompany these issues suggests that concordance stops there. Teacher and principal see each regularity from their own points of view, through distinctive "Swiss cheeses." Rarely are the holes congruent. These kinds of school issues shared between teacher and principal carry potential for mutuality and professional and personal growth. And each carries potential for tension, ill will, and professional and personal dissonance. Most people in schools experience far too much of the latter and not enough of the former. While I know of no teacher or principal who enjoys engaging in battle with the other, I know of few who go through a year without conflict.

It seems that teacher and principal live on the flip sides of the same coin. If one wins, the other loses. If a principal comes out ahead, the teacher is shortchanged. If a teacher does take on the combined third–fourth class, a problem for the principal is solved and a problem for the teacher is created. If no one takes the cross-age class, a problem for teachers is avoided and a problem for the principal persists. Seldom does resolution of important school issues bring teacher and principal closer together. More often the recurring school issues are the occasion for generating suspicion and isolation that produce ripple effects throughout the school—as the discouraged words of one newly appointed principal attest all too well: "The loneliness of the position is more than I expected. I hadn't expected the distance between teachers and between teachers and myself. While I knew there would be some distance, I expected to be playing on the same team and working together. In fact, teachers are not comfortable with the principal entering the coffee room. I find that there are few people to share information with and who seem to have similar concerns and problems."

Need it be so? I am not sure. The structure of schools and school systems seems to discourage openness and cooperation. Principals are accountable to parents, the central office, school boards, and the state department of education. The school principal is the agent through which others seek to prevail on teachers to do their bidding. Principals are judged on the basis of how effectively they can muster teachers to the drumbeats of these others, by how well they monitor minimum competency measures, enforce compliance with districtwide curricula, account for the expenditure of funds, and implement the various policies of the school board.

Principals who take on the role of transmitter to teachers of policy and expectations from others curtail what teachers would like to do, and frequently what teachers are capable of doing. In so doing, a wall is erected between colleagues and adversaries. On the other hand, principals who attempt to insulate and shield teachers from the directives of others, thereby giving classroom teachers room to make important instructional decisions, frequently violate or ignore the mandates of others and place themselves in jeopardy. How is it possible for school principals to at once acknowledge, respond to, and satisfy the imperatives of their many constituents outside the school building while at the same time being supportive advocates and trusted and respected colleagues of teachers inside the building? It is no wonder that few who enter the principalship initially sympathetic to teachers can retain a primary commitment to what they can do *for* teachers when inundated by what so many others expect them to do *to* teachers.

At the bottom line teachers, of necessity, look after their own best interests and those of their pupils. Ultimately no one else will. Principals look after the best interests of all the children, all the teachers, and all the parents—and themselves. In the end no one else will. Unfortunately, in attempting to fulfill their responsibilities and protect themselves, teachers and principals have demonstrated a unique capacity to inflict cruel and unusual punishment on one another. The casualties are personal and pedagogical, leading to parallel play and adversarial and competitive relationships throughout the school. And conflict and tension between teacher and principal exhaust everyone's precious energies, leaving less available for helping students and for improving the school.

A Key to Improvement

If the critical school issues like evaluation and placement are ever to become fruitful occasions that bring teacher and principal together in the service of students and the school—that is, if the capacity of teachers and principals to enrich rather than diminish each others' lives and work is to be realized—conditions must change. Somehow the school principal must assume more of the burden of protecting the best interests of teachers and liberating more of the constructive power of which teachers are capable. In addition, each teacher will have to assume more ownership for the best interests of the school—including other teachers, other teachers' pupils, and the principal. A key to improving schools from within, then, lies in improving the interactions among teachers and between teachers and principals, and it is to this topic that I now turn.

THREE

Becoming Colleagues

I am a beekeeper. I am looking out a window of an 1800 farmhouse in coastal Maine at three hives of Italian honey bees draped under a generous cloak of snow. Last summer I robbed over a hundred pounds of honey from each of these colonies, more than enough to get family and friends through the winter—leaving enough behind for the bees. I remember looking through this same window last summer, pondering these remarkable little creatures and their complex social organization. In a hive of 60,000 or so insects there are scouts always on the lookout in the fields for a new source of nectar about which to tell others through their elaborate dances. Fanners stand on the landing board during a hot day for hours at a time, beating their wings in order to circulate fresh air through the colony. Water carriers find a pond or stream and portage this precious matter back to help cool the hive and process the honey. Nectar carriers bring in the raw material for the honey. Cappers seal the honeycomb in wax and drones mate with the queen and keep the hive strong in numbers.

Observing these astonishing levels and examples of communication, mutual visibility, sharing, and interdependence, I could not help but compare the bees' little society with those we call schools. Perhaps in some ways this is an unfair comparison, but the juxtaposition suggests to me just how much parallel play and adversarial and competitive relationships dominate our schools, how little we see of collegiality, and how much our schools suffer because of it. On the one hand, it is a discouraging realization; but these little honey bees also have a more positive message. They suggest just how great the power of cooperative behavior in the service of a common purpose may be. There is as much to be learned from honeybees as from school sandboxes.

What Is Collegiality?

It's difficult to spell, hard to pronounce, harder to define. It's hardest still to establish in a school. Strangely, collegiality and the ideas it connotes have seldom shown up in the effective schools literature of the past decades. Collegiality is not one of Edmonds's five factors: strong leadership, emphasis on basic skills, a clear sense of purpose, monitoring of academic progress, and an orderly environment (Edmonds, 1979). Nor is collegiality a part of the vocabulary of current national studies of American education. It is recognized neither as part of the problem nor as part of the solution.

I wonder why not. Most probably agree that collegiality in a school is nice, but it is a soft and fuzzy notion at a time when schools need rigor and clarity. Collegiality is nice, but it is a frill when schools need to be pared to the basics. Collegiality is an adult notion, when the lesson plan for schools should be students. And collegiality is nice, but it is perhaps risky. Notions such as these keep schools from investing time and effort in promoting collegial relationships. In fact, I find the least common types of relationships among adults in schools and universities to be those that are collegial, cooperative, and interdependent.

It is important to distinguish between *collegiality* and another word that sounds like it—*congeniality*. Congeniality suggests people getting along with one another. Friendly, cordial associations. Talk in the teachers' room about the Red Sox, Yankees, and Celtics. Discussion about *Roe* v. *Wade* or plans for the weekend. Congeniality. People enjoying each other's company and getting along. Schools need it. Every organization needs it.

Usually, when we refer to "my colleagues" we are, in fact, talking not about collegiality but about congeniality. So what is collegiality? It is the flip side of parallel play. It is not sandboxes, but honeybees.

Judith Warren Little (1981) offers a good operational definition of collegiality in schools. Collegiality is the presence of four specific behaviors, as follows: Adults in schools *talk about practice*. These conversations about teaching and learning are frequent, continuous, concrete, and precise. Adults in schools *observe each other* engaged in the practice of teaching and administration. These observations become the practice to reflect on and talk about. Adults engage together in *work on curriculum* by planning, designing, researching, and evaluating curriculum. Finally, adults in schools *teach each other* what they know about teaching, learning, and leading. Craft knowledge is revealed, articulated, and shared.

I have not seen a better thumbnail description of a healthy school. And yet as obvious and compelling as these professional activities are, they find all too little following. Collegiality is eclipsed by other goals that appear more closely related to the fundamental purposes of schools.

The literature suggests that a number of outcomes may be associated with collegiality. Decisions tend to be better. Implementation of decisions is better. There is a higher level of morale and trust among adults. Adult learning is energized and more likely to be sustained. There is even some evidence that motivation of students and *their* achievement rises, and evidence that when adults share and cooperate, students tend to do the same.

A healthy institution is one characterized by relatedness with other people and gratification from others and from the work itself. If these are among the benefits of more collegial relationships among adults in schools, collegiality may indeed be closely related to the time-honored purposes of schools. And the task of developing collegiality may be integral to the task of improving schools.

Introducing Collegiality in the Schools

Collegiality is nice—but it is extremely difficult to introduce into the persistent cultures of schools. Schools display little collegiality because, like most good ideas in education, it is easier said than done. As we all know, enormous risks and frequent costs are associated with observation, communication, mutual visibility, sharing knowledge, and talking openly about the work we do. Collegiality requires that everyone be willing to give up something without knowing in advance just what that may be. But the risks and costs of interdependence are nothing next to the risks and costs of sustaining a climate of emotional toxicity, of working in isolation, in opposite corners of the sandbox.

Most good schools that I visit are ones where somehow parallel play and adversarial and competitive relationships among adults have been transformed into more cooperative and collegial ones. It *is* possible. Like inner city schools whose students are achieving at a level far above what might be predicted, there are precedents. And, as Ronald Edmonds often said to me and others, "If I can show you *one* school that can do it, it can be done."

I think that the problem of how to change things from "I" to "we," of how to bring a good measure of collegiality and relatedness to adults who work in schools, is one that belongs on the national agenda of school improvement—at the top. It belongs at the top because the relationships among adults in schools are the basis, the precondition, the *sine qua non* that allow, energize, and sustain all other attempts at school improvement. Unless adults talk with one another, observe one another, and help one another, very little will change.

And it belongs at the top because collegiality is not the natural state of things in schools and never will be. It will not occur on its own. A group of graduate students engaged in internships in Boston-area schools compiled two lists: The first included forces (such as an in-school newsletter) they found at work in schools that seemed to contribute to the formation of collegial relations; the second was a list of forces (such as teacher evaluation) observed in the schools that contributed to isolated, adversarial, and competitive relationships. The second list was overwhelmingly predominant. It seems clear that collegiality will come to schools only if it is valued and deliberately sought after, only if someone deliberately takes action to overcome these obstacles.

I do not think that teachers and principals really like to work the greater part of each day swamped by students and isolated from adults, secluded in what one teacher called "our adjoining caves." I do not believe that teachers or principals really teach or learn well in a climate of competition, isolation, or siege. Rather, I believe that one high school teacher speaks for most in saying, "I don't want to get out. I want to get better at what I do along with others who are equally interested in their personal and professional growth."

There is growing evidence that principals who value collegiality can help a school move toward it. Principals may not have tremendous resources at their disposal, but most have more than they think. For instance, Little (1981) found that the prevalence of collegiality in a school was closely related to four specific behaviors of the principal:

1) States expectations explicitly for cooperation among teachers. "I expect all of us to work together, help one another, and make our knowledge available."
2) Models collegiality, that is, enacts it by joining with teachers and other principals working collaboratively to improve conditions in the school.
3) Rewards collegiality by granting release time, recognition, space, materials, or funds to teachers who work as colleagues.
4) Protects teachers who initially engage in collegial behavior and thereby risk the retribution of their fellows.

I find this a powerful little protocol for any of us who would like to have a constructive influence on others.

There are other means within reach to promote collegial relationships. It has long been my belief that the optimal number of adults working together for children is two. One teacher in a self-contained classroom gets pretty lonely and depleted.

Large teams, on the other hand, spend too much time and energy in meetings, trying to achieve consensus. As principal, I encouraged teachers to pair with one another, and almost half of them did. The exchange might simply be, "You take my kids for math and I'll take yours for language," or a more elaborate setup in which the two teachers trade all the time in different subjects. Or it might be that they treat the two classrooms as one large class and divide up their responsibilities. In high schools other possibilities present themselves, such as an English teacher and a history teacher teaming up. Teachers working in any kind of team are provided with a built-in support system, someone to observe and by whom to be observed, an adult with whom to talk about teaching, learning, and students. In short, teachers who work together can enjoy continuous professional, collegial relationships.

And teachers who engage in important school decisions develop collegial relationships. Teachers, of course, make hundreds of decisions each day in their classrooms about supplies, discipline, and assignment of readings. But other important decisions that directly affect teachers' lives are made by someone else. Exclusion from critical choices leads to a pervasive feeling of inefficacy and isolation that erodes the profession. As one teacher put it: "I would not advise any of my children to become a teacher. There is no room to do things that I believe in as an educator." Decision making, on the other hand, bonds the decision makers. Let me give two illustrations of decisions to which teachers can be a party and thereby become colleagues.

Empowering Teachers

Money can be an antidote to a feeling of powerlessness. A little money is a large antidote. Each year our school was allocated about $30 per child for all instructional purposes. I allocated a "fair share" to each teacher—about $750 a year. How this money was spent was up to each teacher; it could go for texts, games, food, teacher courses, field trips, or testing materials.

Seven hundred and fifty dollars is not much, but it is more than many teachers have to spend. It is meaningless to give people responsibility without giving them the resources to exercise that responsibility. In that sense, the money is almost as important as a symbol as it is a means for teachers to buy materials and supplies. It is a vote of confidence. What teachers do with limited funds is what most people do with their budgets; they become responsible and resourceful; they feel empowered. And what most teachers do is to pool their precious resources in order to stretch them further. Joint purchases of books, science materials, and field trips led to joint discussion about these materials, their use and benefit to youngsters. A simple budget and the occasion to make decisions helped generate complex forms of collegiality.

The profession of teaching in colleges and universities and in independent schools does not face the same crisis as that in public elementary and secondary schools. One reason is that professors and teachers there have a greater influence over what they teach, how, and with which materials. Public elementary and secondary teachers have less control over curriculum, but they can have more.

Each June I asked teachers to prepare curriculum outlines for the following year that revealed what they wanted to teach. The outlines might reflect a little or a lot of the system's guidelines, but above all were to be "honest." This practice shifted the teacher's role from passively compliant to actively creative. Although exposing themselves in this way caused both labor and risks, most teachers gladly accepted the accountability, because with the costs came a large measure of control over classroom instruction.

Unlike the system's guidelines, one teacher's curriculum never corresponded neatly with that of another. Their curriculum outlines did not form anything resembling a coherent blueprint for the elementary years suitable for solemn presentation at a PTA meeting. So, each year we selected a different subject—science, for instance—and collated each teacher's plans for the year. A huge poster in the faculty room revealed what each teacher was doing in science; it also tended to show some startling omissions and redundancies. Why was everyone growing bean seeds? Questions emerged. Teachers had to talk with one another, establish some priorities, and make some decisions. The curriculum began to be articulated because the teachers began to be articulate, to be colleagues. Mindless use of imposed curricula leads to sandbox behavior and grit. Active contribution to and creation of curricula leads to honeybee behavior—and honey.

The biggest problem besetting schools is the primitive quality of human relationships among children, parents, teachers, and administrators. Many schools perpetuate infantilism. School boards infantilize superintendents; superintendents, principals; principals, teachers; and teachers, children. This leads to children and adults who frequently behave like infants, complying with authority from fear or dependence, waiting until someone's back is turned to do something "naughty." To the extent that teachers and principals together can make important school decisions, they become colleagues. They become grown-ups. They become professionals.

But the number and nature of the decisions for which teachers and principals have responsibility determine just how grown up they will feel (and behave). There are, of course, many other fingers in the pie. Many outside the school building—in the central office, in the state department of education, and in universities—also want to influence important school decisions such as those concerning pupil evaluation, curriculum, parent involvement, design of space, codes of discipline, and selection of textbooks. And they have just claims. So although there is probably no more fertile, demanding, and satisfying place for collegiality in schools than in sharing responsibility for important decisions, the world out there has other ideas about how these decisions should be made and by whom. In short, just how ownership for school decisions is distributed has a huge influence on the capacity of a school to improve from within.

FOUR

Building a Community
of Learners

When I was growing up on a farm, my favorite companion was a goat. She was smart, friendly, playful, unpredictable, with a mind of her own that would not distinguish between a snack of grass and the carefully tended flowers surrounding our house. She was a most agreeable companion, until confined by a wagon harness, when she became most ornery. In short, our goat asked for a lot but contributed much in return.

A generation later, when my two daughters sought a farm companion, we took on five sheep. They lived happily within a fence, caused little trouble—and brought disappointingly little joy. "Mary Had a Little Lamb" notwithstanding, the sheep turned out to be docile, unaffectionate, and uninteresting. They asked for little and contributed less.

List Logic

Recently, I had the chance to spend some time at the Department of Educational Studies at Oxford University. I went to learn about things in another country, particularly about the professional development of teachers and headmasters. I visited schools and talked with many educators, and I returned from England with new thoughts about education in my own country—and about sheep and goats.

It became clearer to me, while 2,500 miles away, that our public schools have come to be dominated and driven by a conception of educational improvement that might be called *list logic.* The assumption of many outside of schools seems to be that if they can create lists of desirable school characteristics, if they can only be clear enough about directives and regulations, then these things will happen in schools. For instance, the intention of one state legislature is to "identify competencies of effective teachers through research and develop training, certification, selection, and compensation procedures that recognize and support these competencies." These kinds of formulations seem to rest on several assumptions:

- Schools do not have the capacity or the will to improve themselves; improvement must therefore come from sources outside of schools, such as universities, state departments of education, and national commissions.
- What needs to be improved about schools is the level of pupil performance and achievement, best measured by standardized tests.
- Schools can be found in which pupils are achieving beyond what might be predicted. By observing teachers and principals in these schools, we can identify their characteristics as "desirable."
- Teachers and principals in other schools can be trained to display the desirable traits of their counterparts in high-achieving schools. Then their pupils too will excel.
- School improvement, then, is an attempt to identify what schoolpeople should know and be able to do and to devise ways to get them to know and do it.

This conception of school improvement has led to an extraordinary proliferation of lists. Lists of characteristics of the "effective principal," the "effective teacher," the "effective school"; lists of minimum pupil competencies and of behavioral objectives for teachers; lists of new certification requirements, mandates, and regulations. The list logic has begotten a list sweepstakes to see whose is the best list. Advocates argue that their description of a desirable school, their catalogue of the desirable characteristics of schoolpeople, and their prescribed methods for attaining these ends rest on the firmest ground.

These myriad lists are making some valuable contributions. Lists provide a coherent nucleus around which to build a conception of an ideal school. Lists are ready vehicles that enable those outside of schools to approach the important matters inside schools. Embedded in each list is usually some fresh thinking about schools that widens the universe of alternatives available for improving schools. Each list usually attracts a band of believers who will take the next step and employ the list to address the problems of some real schools. And each list that succeeds in improving a single school holds the promise of improving all schools. In short, the list logic of educational change seems simple, straightforward, and compelling. Its only flaw is that it does not seem to work very well.

I suspect that there may be several reasons why this is so. For one thing, the widespread belief that schools and schoolpeople do not have the capacity to improve themselves is not unknown to those who work in schools. Most teachers and principals respond to even enlightened lists not with renewed energy, vigor, and motivation, but rather with feelings of tedium, oppression, guilt, and anger. The vivid lack of congruence between the way schools are and the way others' lists would have them be causes most schoolpeople to feel overwhelmed, insulted, and inadequate—hardly building blocks for improving schools or professional relationships.

The assumption that "strong leadership" and "effective teaching" are whatever brings about high student test scores suggests a very limited—and demeaning—view of both students and their educators. Good education is more than the generation of good scores on tests. Furthermore, what causes teachers and principals to spring out of bed at 6:30 A.M. is not the preparation for, administration and scoring of, and remediation after tests. Tests lead to a preoccupation with production, workbooks, worksheets, and drills, whereas teachers report that the major reward they derive from teaching is promoting, in broader and more imaginative ways, the growth and development of their students.

Lists tend to be prescriptions for other people and for other people's children. Most external lists constitute a suffocating description of a teacher's job, a principal's job, or a pupil's job. They create roles that few of the list makers are apt to want for themselves or for their own children.

Moreover, I doubt that we would find that many teachers, principals, and students in high-achieving schools comply closely with anybody's list. As Ronald Edmonds often said, we know far more about the features that characterize an effective school than we know about how a school becomes effective in the first place. Why, then, do we try to force schools we do not like to resemble those we do like by employing means that have little to do with the evolution of the kind of schools we like?

And finally, I think the list logic breaks down because it depends for its success on the existence of bright sheep. We read proposals every day suggesting ways to attract, train, retain, and retrain the best and the brightest to work with our children in school. Yet, on the very next page, we read more and more demands that such individuals comply with the exacting requirements of externally controlled, predetermined, routinized, carefully monitored jobs.

Only bright sheep can pull that off. But sheep don't come that way, and neither do people. As I learned on the farm, you can have dumb, plodding, pedestrian, undistinguished, compliant sheep—or you can have bright, discriminating, questioning, willful goats. You may have both in one school, but it is extremely difficult to have both within a single individual. To be sure, many successful teachers and principals—goats at heart—report keeping "two sets of books." They keep a close eye on what others expect of them: prescribed curricula, minimum student competencies, criteria against which they will be evaluated. They may appear to meet the specifications of these external lists. They also keep a careful eye on what they want to accomplish in their work, according to their own vision of a good school or classroom. Unfortunately, the dissonance and exhaustion created by merely living with, much less reconciling, these two sets of books too often obliterates any good that might be inherent in either. This leaves many adults in school agreeing with one veteran Chicago-area principal who lamented: "You know what I want to be in my next incarnation? An educator."

Higher salaries may lure some bright young people with high test scores and class rank to submit to the indignities of public school life, but money alone will do little to make working in the schools a satisfying profession. Teachers with responsibilities for dozens of human lives 190 days each year and principals who run complex schools with budgets in the millions of dollars do not want to be run themselves, especially badly. Lists of desirable characteristics can be valuable, but they have been taken too far. Logic has become pathologic.

If this is true, why has list logic remained the driving force in education reform? There are two obvious reasons for this. First, it *is* a logic and is thus defensible at impressive presentations before school boards and state legislatures. Second, it enjoys face validity. As one state education department's list of "the ninety-one characteristics of the effective principal" suggests, lists show that we know where we are going and that we are taking steps to get there. They allow us to determine which individuals and which schools have arrived, and they offer political cover from others higher up in the administrative chain of command. In short, lists promise change, legitimacy, and accountability to an enterprise in need of all three.

Still another reason why list logic seems so compelling is that the alternatives are *not* compelling. Anarchy? Independent schools? Free schools? No schools? Accepting schools as they are? Precious few alternatives to the logic of lists spring to mind. And as long as no other conceptions of school improvement emerge, lists will continue to dominate education reform. The debate will swirl around which elements belong on each list (was "parent involvement" a part of Edmonds's list or not?); which list is best (Bennett's, Adler's, the list proposed in *A*

Nation at Risk?); what is the best way of choosing one list to rely on rather than another (pedigree of the panelists? rigor of the research cited?); and who should make these decisions (superintendents? chief state school officers? legislators? academics?). The list logic conception of improving schools leads us down a very peculiar road indeed.

School as a Community of Learners

It is interesting, in this context, to consider the common instructions given by flight attendants to airline passengers: "For those of you traveling with small children, in the event of an oxygen failure, first place the oxygen mask on your own face and then—and only then—place the mask on your child's face." The fact of the matter is, of course, that the adult must be alive in order to help the child. In schools we spend a great deal of time placing oxygen masks on other people's faces while we ourselves are suffocating. Principals, preoccupied with expected outcomes, desperately want teachers to breathe in new ideas, yet do not themselves engage in visible, serious learning. Teachers badly want their students to learn to perform at grade level, yet seldom reveal themselves to children as learners. It is small wonder that anyone learns anything in schools.

Both within and outside the schools, many educators are growing weary of the logic of lists and would prefer that their own common sense be taken seriously, even honored. Indeed, in a growing number of educational projects around the country, I see the outlines of a conception of school reform markedly different from list logic. The Bay Area Writing Project, now related to a "thinking skills movement," Circles of Learning from Minnesota, the Triad at the University of Connecticut, the Coalition of Essential Schools at Brown University, and the development of principals' centers across the country are all examples of educational groundswells beneath which a common vision seems to lie—a vision of a school quite unlike a center of production where principals, teachers, and pupils fulfill lists.

Those who take part in these and similar efforts seem to value and honor learning, participation, and cooperation above prescription, production, and competition. I see in these kinds of endeavors the concept of the school as a community of learners, a place where all participants—teachers, principals, parents, and students—engage in learning and teaching. School is not a place for important people who do not need to learn and unimportant people who do. Instead, school is a place where students discover, and adults rediscover, the joys, the difficulties, and the satisfactions of learning.

We talk constantly about the importance of student achievement, of teachers' staff development, and of the professional growth of principals as if they occur on different planets during different epochs. In a community of learners, adults and children learn simultaneously and in the same place to think critically and analytically and to solve problems that are important to them. In a community of learners, learning is endemic and mutually visible.

An anthropologist friend tells me that dramatic, profound learning takes place in societies in which people of all ages, generations, and positions—grandmother, father, child, adolescent, hunter, cook—live, work, and learn together simultaneously. The grandfather teaches the daughter. The mother teaches the cousin. Everyone is a teacher and everyone is a learner. In many ways, schools resemble these cultures. Both have many generations living together, interdependently, in close quarters for long periods of time. For instance, this kind of yeasty environment for learning is evident in one primary school in the Boston area that decided to explore the Charles River. Everyone—students, teachers, parents, and administrators—set about to discover all they could about the river. They worked together for a year to learn about the history, biology, geology, pollution, and geography of the Charles—and about the power of collective inquiry. What one person in one class discovered was shared and celebrated by everyone else. They became a community of learners.

I see elements of a community of learners in a nearby

high school in which the principal and a dozen teachers meet each week to share their writing and their ideas and to make connections between their writing experiences and their work with students.

An all-white, fully English-speaking elementary school learned during February that a large number of Cambodian children would enroll in the school in the fall. When the Cambodian children arrived, the school was ready. They were greeted in September with outstretched hands of welcome and friendship and even understanding.

An important story lies behind this uncharacteristic greeting. The parents, teachers, and principal had made a decision that it was critical for *everyone* in the school—children, parents, teachers, custodians, administrators, secretaries, lunch workers—to know who these Cambodian children were, where they had come from, and why they were coming. At the outset, no one knew anything, so for the next four months, *getting ready for the Cambodian children* became the curriculum—in reading, social studies, language arts, science, and art programs. Community was real, and as a result, the experience was vital. Learning had an important purpose. Everyone learned how to say something to the Cambodian children in their own language and also gained considerable knowledge about their cultural patterns and their suffering. As part of their preparation, those in the school learned about prejudice and the harm that prejudice brings to persons who seem different. They also learned how prejudice disrupts communities—in schools and neighborhoods. Their learning had meaning and it made a visible difference. The school had helped the Cambodian families belong. The Cambodians, in turn, had helped this school become a community of learners. Not a bad substitute for the logic of lists.

Many conditions appear to foster this kind of profound learning: acknowledging one's inadequacies, posing one's own problems, risk taking, humor, collaboration with other learners, compassion, the importance of modeling, and the presence of a moral purpose. It is surprising to me how these and other conditions associated with learning attract so little attention from list makers and how infrequently they appear in schools where learning is, after all, supposed to be the dominant feature.

Communities of learners seem to be committed above all to discovering conditions that elicit and support human learning and to providing these conditions. Whereas many attempts to improve schools dwell on monitoring adult behavior, on controlling students, on the assurance of student achievement, and on the visible attainment of prescribed skills, the central question for a community of learners is not, What should students, teachers, and principals know and do, and how do we get them to know and do it? Instead the underlying question is, Under what conditions will principal and student and teacher become serious, committed, sustained, lifelong, cooperative learners?

A community of learners seems to work from assumptions fundamentally different from those of the list makers:

- Schools have the capacity to improve themselves, if the conditions are right. A major responsibility of those outside the schools is to help provide these conditions for those inside.
- When the need and the purpose is there, when the conditions are right, adults and students alike learn and each energizes and contributes to the learning of the other.
- What needs to be improved about schools is their culture, the quality of interpersonal relationships, and the nature and quality of learning experiences.
- School improvement is an effort to determine and provide, from without and within, conditions under which the adults and youngsters who inhabit schools will promote and sustain learning among themselves.

Taking these assumptions seriously leads to some fresh thinking about the culture of schools and about what people do in them. For instance, the principal need no longer be the "headmaster" or "instructional leader," pretending to know all, one who consumes lists from above and transmits them to those below. The more crucial role of the principal is as *head learner,* engaging in the most important enterprise of the schoolhouse—experiencing, displaying, modeling, and celebrating what it is hoped and expected that teachers and pupils will do.

As a participant in one principals' center put it, "Since I've joined the center and given serious attention to my own learning, I've noticed that teachers in my building have become much more committed to their own staff development." Much is important for teachers and principals to know. However, *that* a teacher or principal is learning something is probably far more important to the creation of a culture of learning in a school than any list of *what* a teacher or principal should know.

Teachers in a learning community, such as the Prospect School in Bennington, Vermont, are not "inserviced." Instead, they engage in continuous inquiry about teaching. They are researchers, students of teaching, who observe others teach, have others observe them, talk about teaching, and help other teachers. In short, they are professionals. Colleagues helping one another provides a powerful source of recognition and respect both for the helpers and for those who are helped. And teachers find that, when they engage in serious learning themselves, their students take learning more seriously. As one teacher put it: "Learning is not something like chicken pox, a childhood disease that makes you itch for a while and then leaves you immune for the rest of your life!"

Implicit in many of the lists of school reforms is a vision of school as a place where students learn and adults teach, where the role of educators is to serve, not be served. Because schools and those who work in them are accountable for pupils' achievement and because no amount of pupil achievement is sufficient to place every student in the top half of the class, pupil learning usually preempts adult learning. Yet only a school that is hospitable to adult learning can be a good place for students to learn. A community of learners implies that school is a context for everyone's lifelong growth, not just for growth among K–12 students. Adult learning is not only a means toward the end of student learning, but also an important objective in its own right. Educators would do well to ponder Elizabeth Cady Stanton's injunction that self-development is a higher duty than self-sacrifice.

Many lists pose the questions, problems, and tasks that those in schools are expected to address. Lists have also specified who has responsibility for monitoring these tasks—the state department for school systems, the superintendent for principals, the principal for teachers, and the teacher for pupils. In a community of learners, on the other hand, a different set of relationships prevails. Adults and youngsters often pose their own questions and enlist colleagues as resources to both help answer them and verify the answers.

Educators' preoccupation with lists seems to be bucking increasingly heavy tides these days as teachers and principals, behaving more like goats than sheep, become adept at circumventing prescriptions, and as empowerment, confidence in school-based management, and local decision making increase.

The notion of the school as a community of learners may be moving with a different tide, but it, too, is accompanied by a host of tough questions. How can we overcome the taboo that prevents teachers from making themselves, their ideas, and their teaching visible to other teachers? How can principals become active learners when learning implies deficiency? How can students learn to work more cooperatively and less competitively? Can we have more and higher standards for adults and students without more standardization? In what ways can those outside the schools, by working with those within the schools, contribute to the development of a community of learners? Where do legitimacy and accountability come from? How can we unlock the extraordinary idealism, vision, and energy that are sealed within teachers and principals and students? And how can a conception such as a community of learners avoid becoming yet another set of prescriptions, another list to be imposed on teachers, principals, and students?

However, unlike the problems of transforming goats

into sheep and sheep into goats, I find that trying to answer questions such as these is invigorating both for young people and for the adults charged with educating them. And the process leads to the improvement of our schools. Let us consider some of these questions as we turn to the topic of the teacher and principal as learners.

FIVE

Teachers as Learners

Those who value public education, those who hope to improve our schools, should be worried about the stunted growth of teachers. Teacher growth is closely related to pupil growth. Probably nothing within a school has more impact on students in terms of skills development, self-confidence, or classroom behavior than the personal and professional growth of their teachers. The crux of teachers' professional growth, I feel, is the development of a capacity to observe and analyze the consequences for students of different teaching behaviors and materials, and to learn to make continuous modifications of teaching on the basis of cues students convey. Teachers also need to be able to relate their classroom behavior to what other teachers are doing in their classrooms. Teachers think they do that. Many do, but many do not do it very systematically or regularly.

The Professional Growth of Teachers

Too often teachers do what they did today because that is what they did yesterday or because that is what they think others expect them to do. Just as potters cannot teach others to craft in clay without setting their own hands to work at the wheel, so teachers cannot fully teach others the excitement, the difficulty, the patience, and the satisfaction that accompany learning without themselves engaging in the messy, frustrating, and rewarding "clay" of learning. Inquiry for teachers can take place both in and out of the view of students, but to teacher and student alike there must be continuous evidence that it is occurring. For when teachers observe, examine, question, and reflect on their ideas and develop new practices that lead toward their ideals, students are alive. When teachers stop growing, so do their students.

Unfortunately, schools are seen as places where children learn and adults teach. Because parents, as taxpayers, pay, and teachers, as employees, are paid, we expect that pupils will receive services and teachers will provide them. Teachers get what is left over. And there are precious few leftovers these days. A central concern of this chapter is how the schoolhouse may become a context for the personal and professional growth of teachers.

Most school districts operate from a "deficiency" model of adult growth. Certain skills—writing behavioral objectives, using a new language arts program—are deemed essential for teachers to master by the central administration. Many teachers do not have the requisite skills, so after-school or release-day workshops are mandated to remedy the weakness. Staff development takes the form of workshops done to someone by someone else, as in the verb, "to inservice teachers." Many administrators are discovering what teachers have known all along: When a school or school system deliberately sets out to foster new skills by committing everyone to required workshops, little happens except that everyone feels relieved, if not virtuous, that they have gone through the motions of doing their job. So, by and large, the district staff development activities we employ insult the capable and leave the incompetent untouched.

My experience suggests that the professional growth of teachers is closely related to relationships within schools, between teacher and principal, and between teacher and teacher. I am convinced that great untapped opportunities for the professional development of teachers reside within the school and that the principal can be a catalyst assisting teacher growth. The first contention may be difficult for many superintendents to accept, the second equally difficult for teachers. Teachers favor principals most who intrude on their classrooms least. "Leave me alone, don't trouble me with more demands, and I'll be a happy, capable teacher" is the message. The principal who complies, while perhaps as happy as the teacher with this solution, usually has little effect on teachers' professional growth.

Teachers favor principals least who invade their classrooms, leveling expectations concerning curriculum, teaching methodology, classroom management, or pupil behavior and performance. It is even worse if, having told teachers what to do and perhaps how, the principal periodically checks to see if demands are being met.

It is clear that a principal may have little effect, no effect, or even a negative effect on teacher growth. It is far less clear that a principal can have a positive effect. While there seems to be widespread agreement about the potential for principals' contribution to teachers' growth, a major reason for the existence of teacher centers, for the proliferation of a new cadre of educators called *staff developers,* not to mention rising numbers of teacher dropouts and burnouts, is that school principals have failed to make constructive use of the enormous possibilities for adult learning available in schools. Many principals unwittingly find themselves to be inhibitors, not facilitators, of teacher growth. There are good reasons, of course, for the tensions between teacher and principal, as I have suggested. Is it reasonable, for example, to expect that the principal—the person with the capacity to terminate the professional life of teachers—be charged with promoting professional life?

For a decade I was an elementary school administrator in three schools. During that time nothing was more important to me than trying to vigorously promote the personal and professional development of teachers. I encountered many brick walls. Sometimes I was able to go around, over, under, or even through them. Equally often I bloodied my nose against them. I would like to examine my experience as staff developer and share some personal conclusions at which I have belatedly arrived.

About the time I was beginning as principal to lay out plans for the school and staff, I was planting a new apple orchard on our farm in Maine. I ordered a variety of young saplings—twenty-two in all—each said to be particularly suitable for the demanding conditions that characterize Maine winters, and Maine summers for that matter. I planted twenty trees in a four-by-five array. The two that were left over I planted at the end of the field, where they were less likely to succumb to the summer mowing. I lavished all the care and attention on each apple tree in the orchard that modern agronomy and ancient folklore prescribed. I clear-cultivated. I wrapped each trunk in a plastic shield to keep off the gnawing mice in winter and encircled each tree with wire to ward off the nibbling deer in summer. I pruned and fertilized. I sprayed or did not spray (depending on what I was reading at the time). It was at this time that I began keeping a colony of bees to help pollinate. In short, I studiously provided every form of assistance to my fledgling orchard known to apple tree culture.

I will never forget returning to Maine one August after several weeks away from the farm about five years after I had planted the trees. One of my first walks was to the apple plantation, now in fruition. Two of the twenty trees in the orchard had died. Of the eighteen others, seven displayed no fruit; four had a number of small, gnarled, wormy apples; and the remaining seven revealed a small amount of respectable fruit. I then remembered the two trees I had stuck in the ground at the end of the field—trees that over the years I had all but neglected. I found both dripping with large, well-formed, beautiful apples! I recall all of this because I was struck with the similarity between my success as an apple farmer and as a staff developer.

Teachers, like apple trees, seemed to succeed or fail for reasons quite apart from the deliberate nurturing I provided. Some teachers grew, flourished, and produced; others, mildly and intermittently so; and others' contributions were sparse. And there were two teachers who I am ashamed to admit I had initially written off as so set in their ways as to be unworthy of my efforts. Yet, they inexplicably blossomed in the absence of any direct treatment.

Sometimes it seems like there is no more predictable science of staff development than of apple culture. Despite lists of good ideas that research assures us are associated with success, it is not clear to me what format or activities will have what influence on which members of the species. Despite our most conscientious efforts, often we can be no more sure that logical, obvious steps will lead to fruitful growth than we can be that the absence of such steps will lead to no growth.

A Model of Staff Development

Although I have always been reluctant to label or categorize teachers, in considering staff development I sometimes find it helpful to consider teachers as members of one of three groups:

1. Teachers who are unable and unwilling to critically examine their teaching practice and unable to have other adults—teachers, principals, parents—examine what and how they are teaching. Most schools have a few teachers who appear to go through unexamined motions and who grow defensive if others begin to examine these motions.

2. Teachers who are quite able and willing to continually scrutinize and reflect on what they do and make use of their insights to effect periodic changes. They plan tomorrow on the basis of how things went today. But these teachers are uncomfortable accepting examination of their practice by other adults. A large number of otherwise professionally capable teachers work in schools. They are the ones about whom Dan Lortie speaks when he concludes that "for most teachers, learning, success, and satisfaction come largely from students within their classrooms. All other persons (parents, principal, teachers) without exception are connected with undesirable occurrences. Other adults have potential for hindrance, but not for help" (1975, p. 169).

3. A small number of teachers who are able and willing to critically scrutinize their practice and are quite able and willing, even desirous, of making their practice accessible to

other adults. The teachers in this group are the ones with whom most staff developers, teacher centers, universities, and principals spend the most time. They seek us out, tend to be the most able, and make us feel the most comfortable and successful, although they probably need us the least.

Most attempts at staff development are attempts at group growth. A meeting for the entire faculty is called to induct all teachers in a new form of pupil evaluation. All the fourth-grade teachers in the district attend a workshop on a new social studies curriculum. It is no surprise that most attempts at large-group instruction for adults meet with the same mixed success as attempts by teachers to instruct an entire class of students in a uniform way. If teachers differ in their ability to examine practice and have others examine it, then perhaps our attempts to help them grow professionally should be correspondingly different. The conditions under which each teacher learns are probably as varied as those under which students learn. We hear talk of matching learning styles of students with teaching styles of adults. It would be well to also contemplate the implications of different adult learning styles.

A big part of staff development for me has been an attempt to help teachers progress from group 1 to group 2 to group 3. Group 3 seems like a desirable goal for a number of reasons. Those who exist in this group are often in a state of reduced anxiety, while groups 1 and 2 usually experience considerable anxiety and transmit the anxiety to their students and to other teachers. No one learns very well, or retains very much, or works very long in a state of high anxiety. Anxiety is toxic to the development of community and to learning. And group 3 is a condition in which most teachers are capable of providing or orchestrating a good part of their own staff development, a level of independence from an external "staff developer." And finally, group 3 brings the advantages of collegiality already considered—comfortably giving and taking and working together. Every teacher is a staff developer for every other teacher. This kind of adult interdependence goes a long way toward overcoming the loneliness of teaching.

How does one help a teacher move from fearful and infrequent introspection toward natural reflection by self and others? It is hard, very hard. Many teachers begin their careers right out of graduate school in group 3. They have been trained to critique their lessons. They are accustomed to a supervisor with clipboard at the rear of the room doing the same. Many even grow to like and depend on adult attention and scrutiny. Then something happens that moves the teachers away from group 3 toward group 1. A parent wants to observe her son's reading class on day one. But, when, on day two, the parent writes an angry letter to the principal about Johnny's placement in the bottom group, the teacher is far less likely to welcome adult scrutiny on day three.

A particular problem for the principal who might want to assist teachers in moving from group 1 toward group 3 is that principals are a large part of the reason teachers move from the third toward the first group. How open to scrutiny and how secure can a teacher be when the principal is evaluating classroom performance and making a decision about reappointment? How can one not be anxious and withholding under these conditions?

Like most school principals, I engaged in the formal evaluation of teachers, required each year by the school board. There were several familiar components. First, I observed in the teacher's classroom two or three times during the fall. Before each visit, the teacher and I shared ideas and, after observation, more ideas. Then separately, we filled out the official form, commenting on work in the different subject areas and on relationships with parents, other teachers, and children. After that, we brought the two sets of forms reflecting our perceptions to another conference. I was always particularly interested in differences in our perceptions. When I identified difficulties, I almost always found that the teachers, except possibly those in the first group, were also well aware of them. We discussed how the problems might be addressed. The last step was to incorporate both sets of observations into a final report, which went to the personnel office with a recommendation about reappointment.

In theory, formal evaluation of teachers by principals is a powerful means of promoting professional growth. Indeed it is presumed to be the major means. Many principals use it as an effective way of improving teacher performance—especially when teachers are pushing toward their own goals. On balance, however, I found that formal evaluation had only limited influence on staff development. Its possibilities remained largely unclear and unfulfilled. As conscientiously as I tried to carry out the conventional supervisory duties, I found that they had little impact on teachers' growth. On the contrary, conventional supervision often approaches a meaningless ritual. Or even worse, it becomes a recurring occasion to heighten anxiety and distance between teacher and principal, and competition between teacher and teacher.

Perhaps it is more accurate to say that formal teacher evaluation fulfills many purposes, few of them related to professional learning. Evaluation is often used to induce teachers to adhere to lists or to a prescribed curriculum. Evaluation is frequently organized around the needs of a school system to assemble a competent staff; to determine who should be hired, rehired, promoted, granted tenure, or dismissed; and to convince taxpayers and school committees that the system enforces rigorous expectations and is getting the most from its employees.

Evaluation can also serve the needs of the principal. For some administrators, supervision is an opportunity to exercise "power," to "show the flag," to remind teachers who has authority over whom. For some, it is an opportunity to be accepted and liked by saying favorable things about teachers. For others, it is a means of earning respect for expertise the principal may have in language arts or in classroom management. And, for many principals, the overriding concern during the evaluation process is to avoid conflict—to take an unpleasant, demanding task and dispense with it as quickly and painlessly as possible. That is why so many evaluations of teachers, like teachers' evaluations of pupils, are "milquetoast." They have no sharp edges, distress no one, and settle the stomach.

Too often the system's and the supervisor's needs compete with, and obscure, the most important purpose of supervision: to help teachers learn and thereby to help their students learn. When I began as a principal, I used to think that successful staff development had occurred if teachers did what I expected them to do—follow the curriculum outlines, arrive in the morning on time, and write careful pupil evaluations. But soon I became dissatisfied with this definition. I altered my conception of effective staff development to "do what I expect you to do and do it well." I expected teachers to not only teach about the Navajos but to build hogans with children, to learn Navajo dances, and to write poems about the Navajos.

But still I noticed that some teachers did not seem to care. So my conception of staff development subsequently extended to something like, "Do what is expected of you, do it well, and love it!" I was finding, of course, that while teachers might well follow the guidelines, they did so with all the eagerness of a child confronting a plate of spinach. I then became intent upon finding conditions over which I had control that would make it likely that teachers would conform to my expanded definition of staff development. More disenchantment. Belatedly I began to realize that I was engaging not in staff development, but in promoting institutional compliance—not in the personal and professional growth of teachers but in, at best, "inservice training."

To be sure, if an organization as complex as a school is to survive, it is important that members conform to certain expectations and norms such as teaching literacy skills and coming to school on time. But to make these norms the sole content for adult growth is to prescribe a pretty undernourished diet—to succumb to list logic, in other words.

Over the years, staff development has come to take on quite a different meaning for me. I now see it as listening in a hundred different ways for a question to emanate from teachers. It usually takes the form, "Here's what I want to try." And staff development means being ready to supply assistance or encouragement in a hundred different ways.

Implementing this conception of staff development caused me many new problems: how to encourage teacher initiatives, particularly from teachers unable or unwilling to benefit from others' observations; how to comply with the increase in requests for more resources; how much of the risk I was prepared to share with the teacher if things went awry; and (speaking as an electrician) how to be an "insulator" for teachers from competing demands from the central office, state department of education, and parents, rather than a "conductor" of all of these demands.

I found that any initiative emanating from a teacher, whether a request to buy 1,000 tongue depressors or to deviate from the prescribed curriculum to build a new one based on last summer's trip to Alaska, carries with it a powerful potential for professional growth. The way to ensure that a teacher becomes a deeply engrossed student, it seems, is to allow and encourage the teacher to identify the issue that the teacher will be addressing and to share in the risks of pursuing that issue. The source of the problem for adults, as for students, determines the energy and motivation that will be expended on resolving the problem. Some call it "ownership."

I found that my earlier model of staff development led to some degree of uniformity in school program and appearance (however, not in output), and quite a little group 1 and 2 guarded behavior. Responding to teachers' initiatives, on the other hand, led to wide diversity of teachers, teaching styles, methods, and programs—and considerable interdependent behavior of the kind characteristic of group 3. I found that diversity of teaching, in and of itself, leads teachers to examine their practice more closely. When one teacher is using three reading groups on one side of the hall and another has an individualized program, each teacher begins to reflect on the relative merits of both programs. And I found that diversity can have as much survival value in elementary schools as in graduate schools if what is taught is of uniformly high quality. My earlier incarnation as staff developer was one in which I imposed expectations on teachers, and compliance lasted only as long as I was there to monitor and supervise. Change that emanates from teachers, on the other hand, lasts until they find a better way. And perhaps the most welcome discovery for me was that the life of a school principal who redefines his role as staff developer can become quite rich and satisfying.

I find that staff development is least effective when planned, premeditated, and deliberate. When principals set out to train teachers, run workshops, conduct inservice training, or direct faculty meetings, I see only modest professional change come to teachers. On the other hand, I find professional development most likely to occur as a consequence of teacher and principal imaginatively pursuing regular school issues and functions together.

I have found most successes in promoting the growth of teachers by rearranging the conditions and structures under which teachers work. Because principals can influence many of the elements central to a teacher's professional life—time, coverage, space, materials, money, personnel—they have an extraordinary opportunity to work with teachers to shape a school environment in which teachers become students of their own and others' teaching. Many who have successfully tampered with "the ecology of teaching" have found that a small adjustment to one part of the school culture can dramatically alter the rest of it. I described in *Run School Run* (Barth, 1980) some effects on teachers' professional development that come when a principal deliberately changes institutional condition and structures. Let me give some examples:

Faculty Meetings. We decided to hold each faculty meeting in the classroom of a different teacher. During the first twenty minutes, host teachers told us what they did in their rooms, something about their curriculum, grouping practices, and special characteristics of the class. While initially these parts of the faculty meetings were tense and awkward, the faculty grew more comfortable as both presenters and receivers at these sessions. This rather contrived activity "primed the pump" and legitimized talk about instruction. We moved collectively from group 1 toward group 3. After a few years the practice was abandoned because discussions about teaching had become a customary part of the everyday life of the school.

Placement of Pupils. There was another way in which teachers gave and received access to one another's classes. Students were assigned to teachers each year on the basis of two considerations: Under what instructional conditions does each child in a class seem to work best? And which of next year's teachers comes closest to providing those conditions? To answer these two questions, teachers had to learn to observe each student in the class carefully. And they had to learn something beyond faculty room gossip about how their colleagues taught. Thus, each "sending" teacher spent a half day during the winter observing the classroom of each "receiving" teacher for the purpose of finding the optimal placement for students. After each visit, the two teachers had lunch together. This process, of course, violated the taboo against one teacher invading the sanctuary of another's classroom. I found that exchanging the teachers' problems of isolation for the principal's problems of coverage, checking, and a bit of arm twisting led to better pupil-teacher matches and therefore better school experiences for children, "updated the stereotypes" teachers held of one another, and frequently stimulated ongoing conversations about how teacher A might handle a unique problem of student B. I suspect as much "staff development" emerged from these many visits and discussions as from a year's worth of inservice training.

Schoolwide Responsibilities. An effective administrator makes sure that someone is attending to each important area of school life—either the principal or someone else. I favor someone else. It is impossible for one person to run an institution as complex as a public school. The person who attempts to do it all may get some measure of control and uniformity but pays for these successes with ineffectiveness and exhaustion. When the faculty participates in operating a school, the results are also mixed: frequent disagreement, a lot of careful juggling, considerable effectiveness, a great deal of independence and interdependence training, and not a little professional invigoration.

I enlisted and worked with committees of teachers, fully responsible for decisions over such schoolwide matters as discipline, use of the library, scheduling, and student teachers. Each committee was assured of principal support in advance. A teacher "coordinator" was appointed in each subject to mediate between the central office and the faculty and coordinate curriculum within the school in a particular subject. Involving teachers as committee members and as coordinators had many ripple effects. These formal responsibilities encouraged teachers to relate directly and frequently with one another over sensitive, conflict-laden issues. Teachers learned that assuming responsibility for school problems frequently meant assuming responsibility for one another's problems. The title of "coordinator" not only legitimized this role, but also led to the expectation that teachers would observe and help one another. And both committees and coordinators frequently determined norms of acceptable behavior for teachers. When teachers have legitimate authority, sanctioned by the principal and faculty, they find the courage to make demands on their colleagues in one instance and to comply with their colleagues' demands on them in another.

In this way nonteaching responsibilities become a large part of the life of a school and the lives of teachers. Committees and coordinators thus help to break down the isolation of teachers' lives and of the principal's life as well. This blurring of roles between "teacher" and "administrator" solved some problems and created some new ones, enabling all members of the school community to contribute their strengths and share the power and the satisfaction—as well as the price—of influence. This was another exchange that I feel contributed profoundly to the professional growth of teachers.

Teacher Learning: Summary

Teacher burnout is related to overwork, but as much to the precious little provision in schools for teachers to replenish themselves and help replenish others. Each of these practices suggests that teachers can become learners and can be extraordinarily effective in stimulating and promoting the development of other teachers. Taken collectively, these kinds of practices can have a significant influence on the culture of the school. Each contributes in unanticipated, unplanned ways to the growth of individual teachers and that of the principal. And these kinds of practices suggest that the school principal may be able to provide some of the conditions under which teachers learn. Finally, these experiences suggest that it is possible for a school to make strides toward becoming a community of learners.

SIX

Principals as Learners

The discussion of the school head in promoting the professional development of faculty leads us squarely to the principalship. Is it possible for principals to move away from lists, to themselves become learners, joining with others in building communities of learners?

In the early 1950s, supporters and reformers of public education fixed their eyes firmly on the central administration of local school systems. School boards and superintendents were seen as the most effective agents for change, and the school district was considered the appropriate unit for analysis and reform. In the following decade attention shifted to the federal government, and then to the states, as the agencies best situated to improve local schools. The assumption was that central agencies had enough money, or the right sort of staff, or the moral authority, or more and better ideas. The place of the principal was as "middle manager," responsible for taking the plans of those outside the school and ensuring compliance by those within.

The Importance of the Principal

Today, the individual school is increasingly recognized as the promising unit for analysis and the critical force for change and improvement of pupil performance. One finding that consistently emerges from the recent wave of studies is the importance within the school of the principal. The words vary but the message is the same:

- The principal is the key to a good school. The quality of the educational program depends on the school principal.
- The principal is the most important reason why teachers grow—or are stifled on the job.
- The principal is the most potent factor in determining school climate.
- Show me a good school, and I'll show you a good principal.

There seems to be agreement that with strong leadership by the principal, a school is likely to be effective; without capable leadership, it is not.

For instance, one researcher observed that "In schools where achievement was high and where there was a clear sense of community, we found, invariably, that the principal made the difference" (Boyer, 1983, p. 219).

Attention in recent years has shifted to the school principal because an able principal has the capacity to create conditions that elicit the best from most students, teachers, and parents most of the time. Principals, more than anyone else, can insulate teachers from distracting, outside pressures so that they may devote their finite energies to students. Principals can orchestrate the school's constellation of unique needs and resources so that everyone gets some of what is needed. And principals have the capacity to stimulate both learning and community.

Difficulties That Principals Face

It is much easier to mention such elements as leadership and community than it is to define them for purposes of either research or practice. And it is easier to define them than it is to know how to produce them through training, or to transfer them from one person or organization to another. Lack of specific knowledge about the skills that principals need in order to be effective school leaders exists at a time when many principals are facing dramatic changes in their roles. The authority principals once enjoyed is increasingly shared with school improvement teams, which frequently include teachers, parents, and students; teachers are exerting considerable pressure to control working conditions; the public is demanding more explicit evidence that educational programs are having desired impacts; federal and state legislative guidelines are placing new demands on the principals' time; and dwindling resources for staffing, and for new programs, have meant that principals must do more with less. Other tensions accompany the dramatic influx of immigrants and foreign cultures.

The stress that principals face has increased with the number and variety of their problems. A once very stable profession is now facing unprecedented turnover. Fully two-thirds of the nation's 100,000 principals intend to quit or retire by the turn of the century. More disturbing, the very best principals appear to be the ones most likely to abandon their positions. The commonly cited reasons for leaving the principalship have much to do with the changing realities of being a principal:

Excessive time demands	56%
Stress (emotional health)	52%
Heavy work load	51%
Desire for change	40%
Fatigue	37%
Lack of support from superiors	35%
Courts/legislation	35%
Lack of teacher professionalism	35%
Student discipline	29%
Student apathy	28%

Responsibility for the education and physical safety of hundreds of other people's children for ten months a year presents extraordinary personal and professional difficulties, which take their toll on the effectiveness of school leaders. The bottom line is that the work life of the school principal is depleting. Depletion of leadership leads to depletion of faculty, of the school, of community, and ultimately of the learning experiences of students.

If the school is the most promising unit of change, if principals have a disproportionate influence on the professional development of teachers and the achievement of students, and if principals are so often overwhelmed by the demands of the job, then what should be done differently? There seem to be three policy implications.

Strengthen the preservice professional training of principals. If the work principals do is to be thoughtful and rigorous, then so should the certification requirements and the formal academic course work preparing principals for the profession. Surveys asking successful principals, "What contributed most to your success as a principal?" always seem to find academic preparation ranking at the bottom of the list. These findings suggest the importance of attention to preservice programs for principals. And, indeed, most of the fifty states have dramatically restructured their certification programs for principals in the past few years, and universities in turn have begun to reform their programs for administrators.

Improve the process of selecting principals. With the selection of a principal goes a large part of the control over what that person will do and what the school will become. The maze of committees through which an applicant must now negotiate attests to a growing awareness of the importance of this decision. Recognition of the principal at the education epicenter is leading scores of candidates to apply for a single principalship. Among them will be many who would lead with distinction. Something about the selection process, however, too often seems to eliminate these candidates in favor of others more likely to perpetuate the prevailing culture of the school and school system. Efforts are being made to more systematically identify which applicants might provide the leadership qualities now associated with effective schools.

Increase professional development opportunities for practicing principals. New leadership skills and, indeed, new conceptions of leadership are urgently needed so that principals may effectively contribute to schools. Support is needed to assist principals in acquiring these skills, and in becoming "reflective practitioners," capable of learning as they lead.

My experience as a principal and with principals' centers suggests that a major antidote to the debilitating demands on the principalship and a major resource in building a community of learners is continuous personal and professional invigoration of principals . . . for those of high ability as well as low, those who meet with success as well as failure, and those who have been on the job for twenty years as well as two.

Happily, renewed attention to the professional development of principals is emerging from a variety of sources in many forms: informal attempts at self-improvement through reading, support groups, personal reflection, and writing about practice; university-based course work for principals; inservice programs based within the principal's school district; programs offered by professional organizations such as the National Association of Elementary School Principals, the National Association of Secondary School Principals, and the Association for Supervision and Curriculum Development; programs offered by state departments of education; activities for principals devised by private foundations such as the Danforth and the Kettering Foundations; and the varied activities of principals' centers.

While, as yet, few dramatic success stories chronicle the professional development of principals, there is no shortage of prescriptions. The central office says principals *should* become more rigorous in evaluating teachers. Parents say principals *should* allow each parent to choose their child's teacher. The faculty says principals *should* support teachers in their conflicts with parents. University professors say principals *should* become much bolder and less cautious in promoting good education. And so it goes. Attempts to "train" principals as others would have them be often focus on lists of specific management skills or contemporary issues, oriented toward quick solutions and based on a diffusion model that assumes that awareness of new methods and ideas will automatically lead to their adoption and successful application. But the ripple effects of these training strategies often prove modest.

What the principal needs most is support and assistance. Every principal, novice and veteran alike, is in and out of "hot water" all the time. These situations provide all the ingredients for personal and professional growth: difficulties, a context for resolving them, and a person who really wants them resolved. These moments of conflict hold great potential for learning. What the principal needs is helpful, nonjudgmental assistance in reflecting on and sharpening professional practice.

The principal arrives at the workshop in the use of manipulative math materials in the elementary grades, introduces the workshop leader to the twenty-four teachers, and then says a few things about the importance of Cuisenaire rods and Dienes blocks. After three minutes, when things seem to be under way, the principal rises unobtrusively and tiptoes out of the room to attend to paperwork, phone calls, and other pressing matters in the office.

Unfortunately, the preceding scenario is too often repeated in schools across the nation. As we have seen, one of the principal's most vital and difficult tasks is promoting the professional development of staff members. But "people changing" for principals is even more important and perilous when the people that need to change are the principals themselves.

The Principal as Learner

As learners, principals have a bad reputation. Many in my own school community wondered whether, as principal, I was educable. Parents, teachers, students, central office personnel, and even other principals sometimes had their doubts. Sometimes, so did I. Let me share some very good reasons why it is so difficult for school principals to become learners as well as leaders.

One, of course, is lack of time. "If I participate in that teachers' math workshop, the schedules for next semester and the phone messages from parents will go unattended." Yet we all find time for what is important and comfortable to us. Protesting a lack of time is another way of saying that other things are more important and perhaps more comfortable. Pushed harder, many principals reveal that "the consequences of my *not* engaging in my own learning appear to be far less severe than the consequences of my not answering the phone messages or attending to the kids in need of discipline at my door." When one's own learning is neglected there appears to be no "downside."

A second impediment comes from principals' prior experiences as learners. Most come to new opportunities for learning with old baggage. District inservice training and university course work have often left principals unsatisfied and turned off. Few retain much confidence that staff development will be engaging, let alone helpful, to them in running their schools. Skepticism, if not cynicism, abounds. Principals build up antibodies against attempts by others to remediate them. Many become gifted and talented at resisting fiercely, if covertly, a deficiency model of staff development that says, "Here's what I expect of you," and asks, "How well are you doing it?" Many attend, few succumb, fewer learn. And even if principals have been successfully trained by means of these staff development activities, without feedback and skillful, ongoing coaching little comes of it. Principals find that the linkages between their behavior in a workshop setting and their behavior in a school are convoluted and tenuous indeed.

Third, many principals consider it unethical, if not sinful, to use public funds and "company time" for their own learning. Like teachers, they see themselves and are seen as public servants whose place is to serve, not to be served. The purpose of schools is to promote student learning. Taking money from the school budget to engage in professional growth opportunities is tantamount to snatching bread from the mouths of babes. Think of what the school could purchase with that money—teacher aides, books, magic markers. And think of what you could accomplish at your school during that two-hour workshop! A strong measure of Calvinism remains deeply embedded in the school culture.

Another obstacle to principals becoming learners is that by publicly engaging in learning they reveal themselves as flawed. To be a learner in many school settings is an admission of imperfection, a scarlet letter. One principal told me that, when he left his district to come to the Harvard Summer Institute, another said to him, only half in jest, "I'm glad the superintendent chose the one who needed it the most." Few principals enjoy the respect and authority they desire and need. They can ill afford to render themselves more vulnerable by telegraphing their inadequacies to the school community. Consequently, principals find themselves forbidden not to know. To become a learner is to admit that the screening committee and superintendent made a mistake; it is somehow to suggest that the principal is not one to whom parents can entrust their children. "Principals," as one put it, "suffer under the burden of presumed competence. Everyone supposes we know how to do it. We get trapped into pretending we know how to do it."

Many principals also consider it inappropriate to be a learner. Just as teachers want children to learn but see their own learning as less necessary, principals want teachers to learn but do not feel that a math workshop is appropriate for them. Reform always begins one rung on the ladder below the reformer. The moral order of the school universe places the principal in authority as knower. The principal as learner is out of place. The principal running faculty meetings or answering phone messages is in place.

Finally, if principals do engage in a learning experience and learn something—a new way of thinking about curriculum, a new interpersonal skill, a new idea about improving school climate—they are then faced with having to *do* something with it. They are rewarded for their efforts at learning by additional work. A most curious reinforcement! Small wonder that many principals, contemplating their own professional development, hesitate because they fear such experiences will further deplete time and energy, already in too short supply.

Any one of these impediments to the principal becoming a serious learner is a force to be reckoned with. Together, they suggest why so few school leaders are learners. These road blocks to principals' learning help to explain why, after much fanfare announcing the birth of the Principals' Center at Harvard and a mailing of 1,500 invitations to administrators in the Boston area, only five persons showed up for the first event. And two of us were the staff of the Center!

Given this massive inertia working against the principal as learner, why bother? What does it matter? Why can't learning for the leader be dismissed as another "it would be nice but"? There are, I believe, compelling reasons that make addressing these impediments not only important, but essential to the health of any school, especially to one that would become a community of learners.

Many of the skills recognized as important for an effective principal are *learned* skills. Take, for instance, the effective schools literature. A principal can *learn* how to continuously monitor the performance of pupils; can *learn* how to convey high expectations to teachers and pupils alike; and can *learn* how to orchestrate a safe, orderly environment. In designing the Principals' Center at Harvard, we enlisted twenty-eight outstanding principals in the Boston area to help us. We found that all of them were vitally interested in the professional development of principals—in their own development and that of others. This offered a bit of early evidence that the quality of the school and the learning of the principal are highly correlated.

Learning is replenishing. We deplore teachers who mindlessly repeat every move this year that they made last year. Yet after several years, principals face equally severe tendencies to switch on to "automatic pilot." One of the reasons I left the principalship was a growing feeling that I was becoming a tape recorder, replaying the same tape for the same events each year. I had a tape for parent orientation night, for new teachers, for the parent concerned about Johnny's reading score—for, it seemed, every occasion. It dawned on me that parents and teachers and students deserved more than a tape—and I deserved to be more than a tape recorder, a sure sign of clinical death. The school suffers. Parents suffer. Students suffer. And the principal suffers. Learning is the best antidote to the deadening routinization so endemic to schools.

Perhaps the most powerful reason for principals to be learners as well as leaders, to overcome the many impediments to their learning, is the extraordinary influence of modeling behavior. Do as I do, as well as I say, is a winning formula. If principals want students and teachers to take learning seriously, if they are interested in building a community of learners, they must not only be head teachers, headmasters, or instructional leaders. They must, above all, be *head learners*. I believe it was Ralph Waldo Emerson who once said that what you *do* speaks so loudly that no one can hear what you *say*.

And, finally, the impediments to the leader becoming the head learner are worth confronting and addressing because principals are people. The most noble and distinguishing characteristic of human life is the capacity to learn. Learning is a sign of life. A school can become a community of learners. And principals are as entitled as others to engage in its central activity, whether or not students' achievement scores improve accordingly. Learning is in and of itself a precious value of which too many principals have been deprived or have deprived themselves. Learning is the lifelong expression of our sense of wonder and of worth.

Fostering Professional Growth

Like most who work in schools these days, principals walk a narrow edge between being able and not being able to fulfill their complex job. Exhaustion and discouragement are high; discretionary energy and time are low. In such a climate, opportunities to participate in a new activity, even one addressed to the principal's own renewal, entail risks and demand that the principal give up something to make room for the new activity or else risk becoming further overextended and depleted. A major paradox confronting any who would assist principals as well as teachers in becoming learners in their schools, then, is that professional development is energy and time depleting as well as energy and time replenishing.

Now that links between principal performance and pupil performance are beginning to be forged in the research community and the importance of continued professional education for principals more widely recognized, there is a clear need for more inventive models and formats for promoting their professional growth. Sustaining the development of school leaders is crucial to the quality of life and to the best interests of all who inhabit the schoolhouse—and to their development as a community of learners. Principals, no less than teachers, need replenishment and invigoration and an expanded repertoire of ideas and practices with which to respond to staggering demands. And even more, principals need a clear vision and a sense of their own professionalism. It is to the development of these qualities that I now turn.

SEVEN

Learning to Lead

In order not only to survive but to flourish, principals need to be able to discuss promising school practices without fear of violating a taboo; they need to learn to share problems without worrying about appearing inadequate. They need to recognize that adult learning is not only legitimate but essential. They need help clarifying and becoming confident about their goals, ideas, and practices so they can act thoughtfully.

This constellation of crucial and largely unmet needs led in 1981 to the creation of the Principals' Center at Harvard. Over 100 other centers have been established in the United States and abroad. A National Network of Principals' Centers—with its headquarters at the Harvard Graduate School of Education—now supports emerging and existing centers through newsletters, conferences, an annual journal, and year-long informal interactions.

What Is a Principals' Center?

While there is no orthodox model of a "principals' center," while diversity among centers is part of the energy that propels the Network, the Principals' Center at Harvard shares with others many common purposes:

- To provide helpful assistance to principals and other school leaders that will enable them to become more successful in fulfilling their goals and providing leadership to their school

- To help principals cope with the changing realities of school administration, including increased time demands, collective bargaining, declining resources, and new state and federal guidelines
- To bring together principals from across districts to share experiences, ideas, concerns, and successes
- To identify promising school practices and arrange for principals who wish to engage in similar practices to visit one another's schools
- To encourage the formation of networks among principals, school districts, state departments, private foundations, professional associations, and universities
- To provide a mechanism for practitioners to take responsibility for promoting their own professional growth
- To provide assistance to principals in sharing leadership with teachers, parents, and students within their schools
- To provide a national forum for discussion of school leadership and professional training
- To bring attention to the relationship of principals' professional development to good schools
- To explore new conceptions of school leadership

Teacher centers in the 1960s and 1970s demonstrated that practitioners can take an active role in determining their professional training needs and provide a significant portion of that training. Although principals' centers frequently draw on the resources of universities, central offices, and state departments of education, they too are places where school practitioners play the major role in their own professional development. In short, a principals' center is *principal-centered*. Its activities emanate from the concerns and aspirations of the principals themselves, and its vitality relies heavily on the resources principals have to offer one another.

Like teachers, principals have a great capacity to stimulate professional growth and improved practice in their colleagues because they occupy the same rung on the bureaucratic ladder. They neither evaluate nor are evaluated by one another. In short, principals constitute a potential cohort—a

potential "group 3," in the terminology of Chapter Five.
However, because the culture of schools neither rewards nor
encourages the sharing of ideas and resources among principals any more than among teachers, there is a pronounced
need for a mediator leading toward their professional interdependence.

Principals are capable of interdependence and learning
if the conditions are right. Considering the importance of
the principalship, of the professional development of principals, the lack of success with principals' staff development,
and the host of impediments that prevent leaders from becoming learners, what have we learned at the Principals' Center
at Harvard during the past decade about the conditions
necessary for principals' learning? A major proposition
underlies our efforts: *Principals will be seriously involved in
designing and conducting their professional development.* It is
our belief that the critical element in principals' learning—
indeed in anyone's learning—is ownership. Learning must
be something principals do, not something others do to or
for them. The questions asked at the Principals' Center at
Harvard, then, are the following: Under what conditions
will principals become committed, lifelong learners in their
important work? Under what conditions will principals
assume major responsibility for their learning? And, What
conditions can principals devise to encourage and support
their own learning?

As I have mentioned, our conviction that a principals'
center must be principal-centered led to enlisting twenty-eight
Boston-area principals as designers of the Center. After six
months of deliberations, this group came up with several
building blocks for the Center, each of which, ten years later,
surprisingly is still in place, attached to the cornerstone of
principals' involvement and ownership. Let me share what
these principals put in place.

There are no more important decisions affecting principals' staff development than those determining the content
and format of activities. An advisory board, chaired by a
principal and joined by eighteen other Boston-area principals

and four Harvard faculty members, was established to ensure
that the major voice about the program was the principals'.
Discussions at board meetings follow a common pattern:
brainstorming about issues about which principals want to
learn more (for example, new technologies, dealing with diversity); sharpening questions related to each theme (for
instance, How can a new Apple II be used both as a management tool and an instructional tool?, or How can the principal come to use differences of age, gender, race, and ability
within a school as opportunities for school improvement?).
The board then identifies consultants, university professors,
and principals as possible resources. Then members develop
an idea, select resource persons, and devise formats. Finally, a
staff member of the center, often a doctoral student interested
in the principalship, takes the plan and invites speakers,
secures a room, advertises the seminar, and evaluates the
session.

Many observers initially questioned the wisdom of
turning responsibility for programs over to principals, fearing
that their decisions, like those made by some high schoolers
in an "open campus," might be frivolous. Many feared that
the Principals' Center would offer what principals "want"
rather than what they "need." Conversely, principals were
suspicious that the Center would be a disguised attempt by
Harvard to "inservice" them. Over time, suspicions abated
as principals demonstrated enthusiasm and inventiveness in
planning programs for their colleagues. A list of some of the
themes addressed at the Center would probably pass muster
in most quarters:

Curriculum improvement
Shared leadership
Using and not being used by the national reports
New conceptions of school leadership
Adult development
Staff development within the school
Special needs students and mainstreaming
Gifted and talented students

Dealing with minimum competency requirements
The impact of standardized testing
Issues facing a woman principal
Instructional skills
Proposal writing for grants
Pupil and teacher evaluation
Supervision of teachers
Involving parents productively in a school
Constructing a budget
Decision making
Priority setting
Time management
Dealing with stress
Assertiveness training
Self-understanding
Racial and cultural awareness
Vision

We are finding that principals, like teachers, carry with them extraordinary insights about their work that are seldom explicit for them, let alone accessible to others. The work of the Center is to reveal this abundance of thinking and practice so it may be more widely available to improve schools. We have engaged in a long and difficult struggle against the belief held by many practitioners that one's success in schools is a private matter, best kept from potential competitors or critics. Equally difficult to overcome is the belief harbored by some principals that the knowledge base for improving schools lies more in universities than within themselves. Many worried, for instance, that when principals talked they would reveal, not craft knowledge, but war stories. But more and more principals are acknowledging the importance of what they know and finding ways of making it available and valuable to others.

In our attempts to involve principals as givers as well as receivers, we are finding that the process of being helpful to others is one of the most powerful ways of generating respect and recognition for oneself as well as for those one helps. We find too that often the most sophisticated form of staff development comes not from listening to the good words of others but from principals sharing with others what they know. Every principal I know is good at *something*. By reflecting on what the principal does, by organizing it, by sharing and articulating that knowledge, principals learn.

Principals choose to participate in the Center's activities as members. Each principal decides to spend $120 to become a member for a year and selects events to attend from a list of forty or fifty presented annually. For their membership fee they receive a catalogue and access to activities, several editions of a newsletter edited and contributed to by member principals, a parking permit in a nearby garage, a library card at the Harvard School of Education, and preference for attending limited-enrollment events such as the National Summer Institute for Principals.

Initially, some superintendents offered to subsidize principals' participation if they could decide which principals to send and for what sort of "remedy." Even a PTA offered to send its principal if we would promise to "fix" him! The board has resisted these offers. By placing the decision for participation squarely on each principal's shoulders, we find that those who participate want to participate. Activities are refreshingly free of back-row cynics because with the choice to attend comes an openness to learn. The board remains adamant in believing that if the activities of the Center are worthwhile, people will come.

By the end of the first year, the Center had nearly 100 members, but there was concern that it was becoming an elitist organization for only "the top ability group" of principals. As had been the case with many teacher centers, it appeared that "those who need it the most would not come; those who came did not need to." We have watched and waited. Today the Center has over 600 members, perhaps 10 percent of whom attend each session. Membership has become generally representative of men, women, novice, veteran, elementary, middle, high school, urban, suburban, with a cross section of interests and abilities.

Principals continue to prefer the neutral territory of the university for their activities, finding that a university-based Center provides a protected setting where a secretary is unlikely to intrude with a worried look and a phone message to "call your building immediately." The atmosphere of an emergency room is not conducive to learning. A contemplative place in the ivory tower is as welcome and valuable for schoolpeople as for academics.

The education business seems to thrive as a sorting enterprise, attempting to narrow the range of human characteristics that appear within any group. The board has firmly tilted in the other direction, toward heterogeneity and diversity. Few activities are grouped. Indeed, when more than 200 principals from across the nation applied for the 100 seats at our first Summer Institute, we were faced with the problem of selection. The usual Harvard criteria such as recommendations, transcripts, and test scores were considered—and abandoned. We decided to make these selection decisions each year with the goal of *maximizing* diversity within the group. Sitting in small groups, talking at lunch, and sharing a dorm with other principals who differ markedly in their geographical region, size of school, length of service, gender, race, income, and ability contributes to a powerful and unique learning experience. During the school-year activities, about one-third of the participants in discussions are not principals at all. Superintendents, teachers, board members, university faculty, and graduate students further extend the boundaries of diversity.

For principals there appear to be few alternative solutions to the same gnawing problems. What do I do with a "marginal teacher"? How do I respond to the parent who wants to remove a child from one classroom and place the child in another? We find that the wider the range of participants and the greater the diversity, the wider the universe of new ideas and possible solutions. We ask of differences not how we can "group them out" but rather how we can generate them and make deliberate use of them to promote learning for principals, teachers, parents, and students. A community of learners is, above all, a heterogeneous community.

Too often, attempts at professional development for principals are group activities. The assumption is that all principals need the same skills before Thursday and all will have them after Thursday. However, principals, like other learners, have "preferred" learning styles and different attention spans, interests, and needs. Consequently, the board attempts to vary activities along several important dimensions—for example, those led by principals, Harvard faculty, graduate students, and outside consultants; long-term, one-shot, small-group, large-group, and individual participation; low-risk (large-group addresses), modest-risk (small-group discussions), and high-risk (writing groups, pairing to exchange school visits) activities. Principals match their styles as practitioners and as learners to these different formats. In the process, many learn something about themselves as learners—the conditions under which they learn best—as well as new content and skills.

Principals' centers then attempt to improve the quality of life and learning in schools by encouraging different ways of thinking about common problems; by transforming school problems into opportunities for school improvement; by encouraging clarification of assumptions guiding practice; by offering opportunities for shared problem solving and reflection; and by providing a context of mutual support and trust in which personal and professional relationships may be developed. Many centers rest on similar assumptions:

- The principal is a central figure in determining the quality of a school.
- It is possible and desirable for school heads to be effective educational leaders, as well as building managers.
- The role of the principal and the nature of schools are becoming more complex and problematical.
- Every principal is very good at something.
- Principals have the capacity and need for personal and professional growth—as much after they have assumed their position as before.

- The principal who is a committed learner is likely to
  have a school full of students and adults who are committed learners.

The Impact of Principals' Centers

We often ask ourselves in what ways the Center may be contributing to school improvement and having a demonstrable
influence on pupils. Put another way, what difference does it
make to a fourth-grade youngster in Watertown, Massachusetts, that the child's principal visits the Principals' Center at
Harvard once or twice a month? We suspect it does make a
difference. For instance, we see the crucial influence of principals modeling learning. I visited one principal, a member
of the Center, and as I entered her office was overwhelmed to
see her name on the door followed in large bold letters by her
title, "Head Learner." What a message that must convey each
day to parents, students, teachers, and central office officials!
Another principal observed: "My staff this year is enrolling
in record numbers in the local staff development program.
Whether this is a reflection of my participation in the Center
and my own new commitment to learning, I'm not sure. I
think it is."

"Do as I do" is a powerful formula in transforming
schools from places with older, learned people and younger,
learning people into a community of learners where everyone
is both a teacher and a learner. One principal put it this way:
"At the beginning of the school year, I put together a portfolio of relevant readings for myself and for each teacher. I
have been adding to that portfolio regularly. I've encouraged
staff members to share anything they read that would be of
interest."

Principals are voluntarily joining the Center and attending in large numbers. They report enthusiasm for what they
experience and learn, carry these conversations back to their
schools and systems, and establish their own professional networks. Many transport Center activities back to their own
faculty meetings. In short, most appear to be experiencing

professional growth that releases and generates energy as well as consumes it.

The concept of a principals' center seems capable of providing recognition and a sense of professionalism for principals. Recognition comes from inviting principals to share their craft-knowledge with colleagues, from empowering principals with major decisions affecting the Center, from helping them write about their important work, and from offering affiliation with a major university that enlists them as speakers in classes and as members of committees and that recently has offered faculty appointments to several principals.

Recognition comes to a number of principals from around the country who teach at the Summer Institute. Others serve for a half or full year as visiting practitioners at the Center, contributing their skills to the staff and providing resources to members while they reflect and write about their professional experience. Many of these school leaders return home to establish centers of their own.

Although not part of the original plan, the Center is contributing to the evolution of a community of school leaders in the Boston area. Principals, like teachers, need and treasure collegiality and peer support. Yet, perhaps even more than teachers, principals live in a world of isolation—and sandboxes. There is often a huge distance between adjoining classrooms; the distance across town to the next school is even greater. When principals associate with peers, it is often at an administrators' meeting. But just as it is forbidden for principals to "not know" within their individual school, principals often have trouble "not knowing" with peers. Seldom is time or setting conducive to collegial support or the exchange of ideas and concerns.

As the bridges provided by generic issues begin to transcend professional chasms, members of this community of school leaders are recognizing a shared sense of purpose. Recently, a Boston high school principal was featured in an hour-long television documentary. The next day I happened to be at the Principals' Center and found this program the focus of discussion. Two things were clear: Almost every prin-

cipal had watched and almost every principal had cheered for
one of their own—both unthinkable a few years ago.

Strengthening of collegial relationships, then, appears
to be among the major outcomes for principals at principals'
centers. A decade ago, few suburban principals talked with
urban principals; elementary administration did not talk with
those at high schools, even within the same district; men
administrators did not talk with women administrators; public school personnel did not talk with their private school
counterparts; and no one talked with those in parochial
schools. Now, conversations among these groups in the Boston area are common and infused with fresh vigor, expanding
the repertoire of different responses to similar school problems. And that is the essence of what principals seek as they
strive to improve their leadership. When principals learn and
share their learning with other principals, they not only feel
professional, they become more professional.

We see more and more indication that fostering a culture of reflection, learning, cooperation, and professionalism
among educators outside their schools contributes to a similar
culture among adults and students within schools. Principals
who once experience these qualities do not want to relinquish
them when they enter the schoolhouse door.

School principals have an extraordinary opportunity
to improve public schools. A precondition for realizing this
potential, I believe, is for principals to put on the oxygen
mask—to become head learners. The Center is beginning to
demonstrate that there are conditions under which school
practitioners are not only educable but will take responsibility
for and voluntarily engage in activities that promote their
learning and the learning of others. In so doing, they telegraph a vital message: Principals can become learners and
thereby leaders in their schools.

An outline of a conceptual model for the professional
development of principals is beginning to emerge that is quite
different from the venerable training models of list logic:

engage in practice

reflect on practice

articulate practice

better understand practice

improve practice

If ways can be devised to help principals reflect thought-fully about the work they do, analyze that work, clarify and reveal their thinking through spoken and written articu-lation, and engage in conversations with others about that work, both they and their colleagues will better understand their complex schools, the tasks confronting them, and their own styles as leaders. And understanding schools is the single most important precondition for improving them.

EIGHT

Practice into Prose

Successful staff development for teachers and principals offers activities that vary along many dimensions. One of the most important dimensions is degree of risk. Probably no professional development activity has as much potential for promoting reflection, clarification, articulation, discussion—and risk—as *writing*. Successful writing about practice can be an endeavor from which "everyone wins," and learns: the writer, the reader, and the school.

And yet while writing about practice is a most powerful form of learning and of sharing craft knowledge, it is also undoubtedly the most problematical. Encouraging teachers and principals to want to write about their important work, getting them to write, and then persuading them to clarify and edit their writing and to make this writing mutually visible can be tortuous, as editors of professional journals such as *Educational Leadership, Principal,* and *Phi Delta Kappan* can attest. In this chapter I want to examine writing about practice for the great promise it holds for improving schools from within.

Obstacles to Writing

Many difficulties accompany professional writing for most practitioners. Anyone who chooses to write about schools and school life must be prepared to face staggering obstacles. Consequently, writing about the practices and problems with which school practitioners deal intimately each day is often left to others. Paradoxically, those who systematically examine and write about schools come, for the most part, not from the school community itself but from higher education.

For scholars and researchers, schools can be frustrating social institutions. Attempts by university people to find meaning in school life run up against a host of well-known impediments. Gaining physical access to classrooms and schools that reject foreign bodies with defiance is one such problem. Getting inside "the culture" of a school or classroom is another. Often researchers find themselves on the outside looking in, drawing inferences about school behavior but seldom having access to parents', principals', teachers', and students' innermost thoughts and motives.

A recurring problem for researchers is corroborating written observations with schoolpeople. The scholar who checks findings with schoolpeople risks offending teachers, principals, and parents whose perceptions of reality are invariably violated by the researcher's account—any account. The researcher who does not convey findings to the adults in the school risks joining the tainted cadre of outsiders who take advantage of schools for their own professional purposes and run, leaving behind little benefit to the school in return for the precious energies that practitioners have invested in the study. In short, schools present university researchers with a murky quagmire. Few scholars manage to serve both the academic community and school practitioners well.

If those who are foreign to the school culture have difficulty gaining access to its innermost secrets, and if this information is important to so many, then why don't practitioners themselves study and write about their school worlds? It would seem that writing about schools as an "insider looking in" offers unusual opportunity for insight into public education. Obviously, teachers and principals have constant access to classrooms and a school setting, not to mention their own ideas, motives, satisfactions, and methods. And the practitioner-author acquainted as colleague or trusted friend with parents, administrators, and teachers would be assured of a sympathetic, even grateful audience. In short, one might suppose that practitioners who write about schools would encounter few of the constraints so familiar to university researchers. So it would seem.

As the author of a book (*Run School Run,* 1980) about my experience as principal of a public elementary school, I can testify that quite the opposite is true. In the preparation of that book, I became all too familiar with some formidable obstacles facing a school practitioner who attempts to write about schools. Some of the difficulties are familiar to university researchers. Others may be peculiar to school practitioners. Together, they suggest why so few schoolpeople write about their work. And they constitute a large agenda for those in principals' centers, universities, staff development programs, and elsewhere who would assist school practitioners in writing.

Time Constraints. First, there is the obvious constraint of time. Writing takes time, lots of it. The university researcher, of course, works under time limitations, but within the university culture one is paid, allotted time, rewarded, and promoted for scholarly reflections and writing. This is hardly the case for teachers and principals. For any "free" or unaccounted time in schools there are a thousand things related to the job that a practitioner should be doing. A principal or teacher feels at liberty to take notes, organize information, make outlines, and write and revise drafts only when the "desk is cleared" of other obligations, which, of course, never happens.

My own vivid recollection of writing while running a school suggests that time for writing comes, if at all, out of my time, not company time. When I did find time, it was on a Saturday morning. But even then I found, as doctoral students writing theses in education find, that wallowing in, reflecting on, and trying to untangle school issues and the inscrutable behavior of colleagues is taxing. One can only take so much. On weekends and holidays most adults (and probably children) who work in schools badly need detachment and relief from their intense work. It is no more reasonable to expect a teacher or principal to spend the weekend writing about schools than to expect an air traffic controller to spend the weekend on a simulator, analyzing hectic airport traffic patterns.

So the problem for the practitioner-writer is not only finding enough time, given the intense and demanding nature of school work. The problem is to identify for oneself and supply the conditions under which it becomes likely one will write. I have found conditions that support my writing exacting and difficult to provide. I needed a year's leave of absence, a foundation grant, and a secluded farm in Maine to say what I wanted to say. I needed another year to edit it and say it the way I wanted to say it. Seven hundred days to write three hundred pages! And I needed the greater part of a third year to solicit criticism and shepherd the manuscript through the stages of publication. Few practitioners enjoy conditions like these that would permit, let alone encourage, them to write.

The Complexity of the Subject. A second obstacle I encountered was the complexity of the subject. What happens in schools—even very good schools—is often illogical, irrational, and unplanned. Effective written language, on the other hand, is essentially logical, rational, linear, and deliberately planned. How do you transform the former into the latter? How do you convert into organized language the massive, simultaneous onslaught of complex individual and institutional behavior that bombards school practitioners each day? Schoolpeople have ready access to an extraordinary source of rich data, but few have at hand organizing principles that allow them to collect, organize, and find meaning in an overabundance of apparently random information. *Conceptual frameworks,* as we call them in universities, are hard to come by.

My own strategy emerged pragmatically. As a principal for ten years, I collected. Whenever something especially noteworthy or problematical occurred—a particularly successful meeting, a remarkable change in a child, a heated letter from a parent, a sudden insight from a teacher—I jotted it down and added it to the sedimentary deposit forming in the bottom drawer of a desk. I set out for the Maine farm with three bushel baskets of these anecdotes and incidents. For two months, I played card-sorting games: I placed each item in a variety of shifting categories until some piles persisted and each piece of paper came to rest in an accommodating category, or in the wastebasket. Each of the enduring piles then became the basis for a chapter in the book.

Within each pile I shuffled, arranged, and rearranged until I was able to find, or impose, some meaning. I have a dreadful memory that seldom allows me to recall names and events, let alone details. But I found that each item I had squirreled away gave rise to a train of associations and rich reminiscences with which I was able to recall the details of long-forgotten incidents. This inadvertent strategy enabled me to convert the raw data of school life into a more or less ordered language. Other practitioners discover other means. But many remain baffled by the distance between the rough, disordered school experience and the polished written word.

Fear of Writing. A third difficulty for practitioners who attempt to write about their school experiences is one shared by those who attempt to write about almost anything—fear, often terror, of writing itself. There is an abundance of craft knowledge within the schools, every bit as prevalent as war stories, but it is not easy for most to separate the craft knowledge from the war stories. Far more critical than insufficient time in discouraging practitioners' writing is the underlying fear that "I have nothing to say," that "others will criticize what I write," that "my writing will neither be accepted nor used by anyone."

These fears of rejection are well grounded. They are the fears of second graders, seventh graders, and college and graduate students—fears of being demeaned by papers returned so marked up by corrections that it appears a bowl of spaghetti sauce has been spilled on them. The criticism, the red pencil, the ridicule of having a paper read before the class, the low grades, all leave permanent scars that inhibit adults' writing. Poor instruction in writing by one generation of teachers produces fearful writers among the next.

Effective writing requires both competence and confidence, which our formal education system often does more to extinguish than cultivate. For many practitioners, then, the fear of being judged an inadequate writer (and, therefore, an inadequate person) is realistic. Consequently, although there are many distinguished teachers and principals, few are distinguished writers. Many are dreadful writers. Almost all experience a monstrous gap between the great deal they know about educational practice and a limited capacity to express this knowledge in writing.

The terror of writing presents a particular burden for schoolpeople responsible for teaching precise writing to students. Teachers and principals are expected to be accomplished writers themselves, or else how could they teach students to write? Publicly revealed incompetence in writing is, therefore, not only a personal admission of failure but a devastating professional indictment as well. No wonder teachers resist pupil-evaluation systems that require written comments to parents. No wonder principals say as little as possible in PTA newsletters!

The Problem of Generalizing. A fourth difficulty practitioner-writers encounter is the problem of generalizing. Writing about what happens in schools is an attempt to assemble and organize information and depict reality as one person sees and experiences it. The university researcher may study one classroom or school at a time but usually bases conclusions on larger samples, thereby gaining credibility and perhaps the capacity to generalize. But many school practitioners have never worked in more than one school. What a teacher or principal writes about is often based on a restricted and nonrandom sample—one teacher, one classroom, one school.

There is seldom agreement about what constitutes "reality" in a school, whether it be the effect of a new language program or a description of how the faculty meeting went.

Schoolpeople, like others, tend to reconstruct experiences, and their own places in them, in very idiosyncratic ways. Often we need to emerge from the drama of school life as heroes, and our accounts tend, therefore, to glorify us. If we acknowledge our limited sample, our bias, and qualify our observations as "one person's view," we can counter the alternative interpretations of others. But if this disclaimer is employed, then the wider usefulness of the account is brought into question and frequently diminished. We wonder who wants to read (or publish) a precious case study by one teacher about one classroom that perhaps has little or no bearing on any other? If there is to be an audience for a practitioner's written account, the writing must have some elements that can be generalized to other situations.

I suspect most practitioners, like university researchers, hope and believe that what they write *will* have value beyond the particular situation. For the university faculty member, this aspiration is acceptable enough. But the desire to generalize, to "stick out" and be recognized, leads the school practitioner up against another obstacle—the taboo within the school culture against distinguishing oneself, or even appearing to distinguish oneself, from colleagues.

The practitioner who writes is haunted by the question, "Are my experiences, ideas, and accounts sufficiently noteworthy to be of interest and value to colleagues?" If the answer is "No," then, at best, one encounters mental blocks before the typewriter and, at worst, ends up spending Saturday morning taking the kids skating. If the answer is "Yes, I know something others don't, or can do something others can't," then one has indeed attempted to distinguish oneself from colleagues and is, therefore, subject to the penalty for violating the taboo. "Who does he think he is, anyway?" "What's so great about that?" "It's pretentious." "I do that all the time!" These "put-down" responses of colleagues are further aggravated by charges of exploitation. "I could write, too, but I am too busy doing what I am supposed to be doing—working with children or helping teachers."

The school practitioner who writes, then, can expect

little support and recognition from others in the building. The culture of schools places little positive value—and often places negative value—on teachers and principals using their positions as participant-observers to write about practice. To write is to reveal oneself. So, many schoolpeople do not write for the same reason they construct walls in open spaces: in order to conceal themselves.

There is another issue concerning generalizing. American education, like social science research, seems preoccupied with a search for "the one best system." Examples of good practice are often scrutinized less for their particular merit than for the answer they may provide to generic problems. I can write about how we reduced discipline problems in one school; readers want to know how to reduce discipline problems in all schools. But whether a practitioner intends to generalize or not, it is unclear whether one individual's observations, interpretations, and conclusions can be more widely applied. Suburban to urban schools? Elementary to secondary? Public to private? Only with great care. In my book, I sidestepped this question by suggesting that problems of education are generic, while solutions to these problems are particular and unique to each context. Furthermore, I placed the burden on the reader to determine which, if any, parts of my account of one public elementary school might be generalized to other settings. I had my hopes, but I made no claims.

Interpersonal and Political Problems. The practitioner-writer faces a variety of interpersonal and political problems. Writing about practice invariably means writing about other people—parents, teachers, students, and administrators. Even more than university researchers, the practitioner must be prepared to share findings and manuscripts with schoolpeople. But in addition, the practitioner must live each day with the consequences of what is written. Teachers and administrators who write about their work must assume that everyone in the school will read what they write, whether they do or not.

Usually, the worst fate that befalls the university researcher whose classroom-based findings are deemed offensive is to become a persona non grata in that school. But these difficulties are eased by time, distance, and the availability of subjects in other schools. School principals or teachers, on the other hand, live in a fragile world. For them, there are no other schools. To write anything at all is likely to offend someone and thereby to foul one's own nest. Most already have plenty of unmanageable problems. Why generate additional problems unnecessarily? In short, for schoolpeople the consequences of writing about practice are immediate and lasting, impinging on those upon whom they must depend for effectiveness and satisfaction. Thus, the teacher or principal who writes about a school setting must decide whether to "tell it like it is" and risk offending others, or launder and disguise the account so it will be unlikely to offend others— and probably will be unlikely to interest others either. It is no wonder that Henry Kissinger, Jimmy Carter, Ronald Reagan, and others write about their professional experiences only after they have removed themselves to a detached and sheltered place!

Legal Problems. Finally, there are the legal problems of the practitioner who writes for publication. One might expect that teachers and principals would have little difficulty gaining permission to use the information so freely available to them. It came as a surprise for me to learn from Harvard University Press that I could not quote my own work. The editor's letter said, in part:

Dear Mr. Barth:
Only a few excerpts in the text belong in the category of "fair use"—those passages that come directly from previously published sources. They are fair use because they are under 250 words in length (which is the approximate criterion for any work of substantial length) and you have given them proper citations. No permission is needed to include these passages in your book.

However, if you want to quote works like letters or poems (or any very short works) either in whole or in part, whether or not a citation is given, permission is required. This applies to all of the letters which were written by parents from your school, numbering around 70-80. You hold no claim to these letters, even though they were addressed to you—and disguising the names of the authors is irrelevant.

In dealing with these letters, you have three options: (1) You can quote directly from the letters and get a signed form from each author (a sample of which is enclosed), giving permission for use in your book. In this case, you should probably keep the names disguised anyway; (2) You can paraphrase the letters in the text, being very careful not to quote directly; (3) Or you can create fictional parents who express similar viewpoints in language that is distinctly different from the language in the actual letters. In this case, you should include a very clear statement in the preface that all of the people represented in your book are fictional.

In any case, please be aware that you are solely responsible for making the manuscript legally suitable for publication—which means picking out the problem passages, and either deleting, revising, or doing the paperwork necessary to let them stand. Should you decide to obtain permission for any or all of the cases involved, the necessary forms and explanatory sheets are enclosed.

So much for the parents' letters. Now we come to all the works written by employees of school systems—superintendents, principals, teachers, etc. Permission to quote from a letter by a Newton teacher, for example, does not come from that teacher if the letter was written in an official capacity. Such works are termed "works for hire," which means that all rights to an official work belong to that organization for which the work is created. I'm sorry to say that even all of your own PTA newsletters, memos, letters to parents or school per-

sonnel, minutes from meetings, personal notes taken at
meetings, etc., are works made for hire. You must obtain
permission from the school boards involved before we
can publish any of these documents.

The fact that all of the information that school practitioners gather or generate as part of their regular working
day belongs to the school board, while understandable, is
sobering. If I have to run a gauntlet of central office administrators and school board members before I may use for publication even my own memos to faculty, it clearly becomes less
likely that I will write for publication. It certainly becomes
less likely that what I do write will contain the seamier (and
more interesting) anecdotes and insights, for who would give
permission for me to use information that might reflect unfa-
vorably on them or their system?

These, then, are some of the constraints I encountered
while writing *Run School Run* (1980). I suspect these are also
among the reasons other teachers and principals find it difficult both to practice and to write about practice. While
"I don't have time" may be the most commonly verbalized
impediment to writing, I find lack of time hardly the most
discouraging element—as other practitioners who do have
time could attest. Taken individually, these many sources of
resistance might not curtail writing; taken collectively, they
have the effect of discouraging writing and reducing the likelihood that the rich information and insights of the school
practitioner will ever appear on the printed page, where they
may be useful in improving schools. Converting practice to
prose is not easy.

The Satisfactions of Writing

Given this rather discouraging picture, why do *any*
school practitioners write? What satisfactions can compen-
sate for these hurdles? Teachers and principals find many
satisfactions.

Personal Recognition. A primary motivation is the satisfaction and recognition that come from seeing one's ideas in print and knowing that others will also. Writing about practice lends legitimacy to both writer and practice. Most schoolpeople feel that education is an important, worthwhile endeavor, but cannot help but be influenced by society's low regard for their profession. In the view of many, education is important but not quite important enough. Being a teacher or principal "and" a writer is more prestigious than being "just" a teacher or principal.

Writing about practice can help the profession as well as the author. Practitioners can communicate the complexities and the successes that characterize life in schools to cynical taxpayers as well as to interested colleagues. Statements by schoolpeople are curiously, and unfortunately, lacking from the ongoing debate about American education and how to improve schools. Yet, who has more to say on the subject?

Sharing and validating educational ideas with other practitioners have additional benefits. The teacher who reads what another has written finds an extended universe of ideas, materials, and methods from which to choose in responding to daily instructional challenges. Written insights have a "memory"; they can subsequently be drawn upon. Insights not recorded vanish. Principals who read what a colleague writes find it easier to order their own school worlds. In short, a writer's description of practice can inform and dignify all practice, while at the same time confirming for each reader that, "God, I'm not crazy, nor am I in this alone."

Tangible Rewards. Another satisfaction for the practitioner-writer comes from the very tangible quality of writing itself. Those who work in schools can never be certain whether teachers, students, parents, curriculum, or "school climate" are better off in June than they were in September because of their efforts. This is frustrating, to say the least. There is something very concrete, on the other hand, about a published manuscript. You can see it, touch it, feel it. What was a blank page is now an article. Certainty of accomplishment stands in welcome contrast to the uncertainty and diffuseness of school life. I find myself enjoying many of the same satisfactions from writing as from shingling a barn. At the beginning of the week the roof was unshingled; at the end of the week it was shingled. It is better than it was, and I did it.

The Clarification of Practice. A third positive outcome I find in writing is the power it affords to clarify practice. In order to translate the disordered, irrational world of schools into the logic and precision of language, one has to organize and analyze what one does and sees in schools. Bringing a higher level of clarity to school work is a luxury few schoolpeople enjoy (and few can do without) in these days characterized by sheer survival. The act of making one's thinking accessible and comprehensible to others also makes it accessible and comprehensible to oneself. A reflective capacity is a condition for personal and professional growth. Thus, by helping to order the disordered, writing supplies a powerful catalyst for professional change and personal growth.

For many practitioners, writing about their work enables them to stand and to withstand practice. Without periodic opportunities to look with detachment at the consuming world of school life, teachers and principals find themselves consumed by it. Writing helps to objectify practice and to distance practitioners from it, and offers a personal nourishment that can energize schoolpeople through the many bleak moments of school life.

Thus, many practitioners find writing about their work a kind of job-related moonlighting, the fruits of which can be channeled back into their work, making it more considered, perhaps more tolerable, certainly more effective, and maybe even easier. The labors of the weekend at the typewriter frequently pay off on Monday morning in unpredictable ways.

There is some indication that when teachers and principals write about their work, students may benefit as well.

Seymour Sarason puts it this way: "The more a teacher can make his own thinking public and subject for discussion . . . the more interesting and stimulating does the classroom become for students" (1982, pp. 185–186). Students benefit from the power of adult modeling of desired behavior. Donald Graves (1980) points out that there is no better way for adults to impart the importance and the skills of writing than to be writers themselves. Graves reasons that we cannot expect a teacher to practice the craft of teaching writing who does not practice the craft of writing itself.

The principal who is preoccupied with control over supplies, reluctant to give teachers magic markers and masking tape, begets teachers preoccupied with control over supplies, reluctant to give students magic markers and masking tape, and students who go without magic markers and masking tape. In the same way, through this mysterious process of modeling, the principal who writes often and with care may find teachers who write more often and with care, and, consequently, students who do the same.

I always thought that the hours I spent writing a single paragraph each week for the school newspaper conveyed some unstated messages to the school community: "We value precise, effective, entertaining written language here and we are working hard to develop it." There were many ripple effects. Teachers struggled over their written pupil evaluations, and I made the struggles no easier by brooding over their drafts as I would term papers. But teachers' communications with parents became more insightful and entertaining as well. I would like to think that confidence in us went up. I am convinced that adults who write well in school, and make their writing visible, teach students as much about writing as those who deliberately set out to teach writing.

And I have found that writing about practice is immensely helpful in speaking about practice. The skills and ideas exercised in writing are easily, if not automatically, transferred to speaking. Most teachers and principals are regularly called on to display the latter skills even though they may not appear to need the former. I find that prior experience writing about a topic contributes to command over the spoken word.

"Leaving Our Mark." Finally, for the practitioner-writers, like many other writers, the psychic energy to stay up all night crafting a manuscript can come from the simple yet mysterious desire for immortality. Many of us, I am sure, have the desire to "leave our mark" that will persist long after we are gone. For many parents, this comes through the children they rear; for architects, through the buildings that endure. For teachers, the "mark" might be the scores of children they have influenced. For a principal, perhaps the "mark" is a school, a collection of teachers, a community that have all somehow been shaped by the administrator. And for some, promise of immortality lies with articles in journals, books on shelves, and entries in bibliographies that will persist long after author and word processor have ceased to function. We entertain the fantasy that somehow, somewhere we may touch and profoundly influence another practitioner in the way a particular piece of writing has influenced us.

Summary

Writing about practice offers something of immense value to readers as well as to writers. I believe the writing many practitioners do represents a legitimate kind of research. It may be questionable whether anecdotal experiences of school practitioners are generalizable to other settings in the way that traditional research findings may be. And it may be that practitioners' writing is often more an exercise in the personal and professional development of the author than a creation of new knowledge. Yet large-scale social science research is often dependent on huge sample sizes that tend to obscure the rich meaning of individual cases. A need exists for investigation of individual cases as well as the aggregate of cases. As my colleague Vito Perrone, Director of Teacher

Education at Harvard, commented to me some years ago, "The individual case informs: Collections of cases enlighten."

Recording examples of successful practice and documenting the process of education as it occurs is data collecting, which is desperately needed to fill out—and sometimes correct—the picture that more elaborate and systematic research only begins to paint. A discussion of standardized tests as they are used and abused in a particular school can shed as much light on the decline of test scores as an elaborate study conducted by the Educational Testing Service. In short, good writing by practitioners about practice is not only personally satisfying and professionally rewarding, but offers a rich contribution badly needed to balance the literature of educational research. Policymakers and school practitioners need access to both.

The work of particular teachers and principals is seldom visible to the public or even to other teachers and principals. One way of making it more so is through writing. Writing about practice is both visible and collegial. It helps build a community of learners. Yet few educators speak out for the abundant accomplishments of schools. Many students out there are learning and achieving, thanks to many school-people who are teaching and leading. No one else can tell the story in the same way. Practitioners who work conscientiously to convey their ideas in print have an opportunity to convey to the public the message that schools are complex institutions; that leadership and teaching are difficult; that more good than bad things are happening in classrooms; that good schools do make a difference for students, their parents, and professionals alike; and that it is quite possible, even common, for schools to improve from within.

I recently had lunch with a friend who, for a dozen years, had been editor of a national educational journal. I asked him if he could put his finger on the characteristics of authors of the very best pieces he had published over the years. Without hesitation, he replied that these are people who clearly know a great deal about education and schools. In addition, they write with great detail. Each has a rich lore of anecdotes and examples to support generalizations. Moreover, these are people who care passionately about their subjects, and this passion shines through their writing. If these are indeed the important characteristics of good writers about education, they are also the characteristics of scores of school practitioners. Who knows in more detail and cares with greater passion about what goes on in schools than teachers and principals?

NINE

Between School
and University

I have spent thirteen years of the past quarter-century as a public school teacher and principal and thirteen years in universities as an administrator and faculty member. Many of those years have been spent at the intersection of school and university, rooted in one while making occasional forays into the other. They are two peculiar cultures, and where they meet is even more peculiar—a rather messy and often quite lively place.

Poor Relations Between Schools and Universities

In the current climate of renewed interest in improving schools, many in higher education are again asking, "In what ways can we use our limited resources to address the unlimited needs of public education?" Attempts by university people to work closely with schools seem to run headlong into a number of painful impediments. Unless these issues are addressed, the good intentions of higher educators may never have an impact on the schools. I do not think that further research is needed to identify many of the difficulties universities encounter when interacting with schools. Drawing especially on my experiences over the years with the Principals' Center at Harvard, I would like to acknowledge some of these impediments and the questions they pose for school reformers.

"Scorned Lovers." As much as we might like, a university cannot mount a new activity with schools as if the slate is clean of old activities. It is not. In their careers, few elementary and secondary educators have escaped being demeaned by universities. Expectations have been held out and violated at the preservice and inservice levels and in courses, workshops, consultations, and evaluations. I will not soon forget the anxiety in the air when we invited those twenty-eight Boston-area principals to serve on the committee planning the Principals' Center. One said, "Harvard makes me feel like a scorned lover." And another, "You people from Harvard have come before. You just ask a lot of questions, then leave and write a lot of criticism. You don't help, you just take our time." Eventually, all twenty-eight accepted our invitation and did indeed plan the Center—but not before we all wrestled painfully with the baggage of the past.

And I know of few university faculty members who have worked closely with schools who have not at one time been badly scratched up in the briar patch. Schools are unforgiving, inhospitable places for academics, where foreign bodies are rejected as a human body rejects an organ transplant. The recognition that professors may enjoy within the ivory tower seldom accompanies them into the schools.

What this means is that both school and university people come to new conversations harboring antibodies that each has built up to protect against the other. It seems to many in the university that schoolpeople want to improve things without changing them very much; from the point of view of schoolpeople, university folks offer to change things but without improving them very much. These are hardly promising conditions for a marriage. The implication is clear: Before launching any new crusade, we must deal with wounds of previous crusades. How, then, to start afresh when burdened with so much bad baggage?

Who Takes the Initiative? A second roadblock to university-school engagement is the little dance we seem to perform around the question, "Who initiates and who responds?" There was a time, I suppose, when it was accepted that universities took the lead by posing the questions, generating the ideas, diagnosing the problems, and offering the prescription. People in the schools responded—or didn't. Nowadays, each is more cautious, preferring to have the other's cards on the table first. The university says, "Tell us what you need and we'll see if we can or want to provide it." Schoolpeople say, "Tell us what you've got and we'll see if we want any."

For the academic, taking the initiative carries the risk of being prescriptive. Bare mention of words like *training* and *should,* or talk of inservice activities and consulting, causes many schoolpeople to bristle defensively. Yet neither academics nor schoolpeople long withstand the former playing the role of teacher aide to the latter. And there are risks in trying to fudge the distinction between being prescriptive and being responsive. The mixed messages lead to the experience many of us have encountered: We conduct an elaboate needs assessment and design an activity to address those needs—and then only five people show up.

Muted Voices. A third roadblock in arranging a marriage between school and university is found in the muted voices of schoolteachers and administrators. As I have suggested, professional journals and research agendas are dominated by university voices and, all too often, conversations between university and schoolpeople (especially when held in the university) are also university-dominated. It is tragic that teachers, principals, counselors, and parents have yet to join more fully in the debates swirling around the current reports on American education. It is unthinkable that any other profession undergoing close scrutiny by so many would find description and analysis of practice, and prescription for improving practice, coming largely from outsiders looking in. Where are the voices of insiders looking in?

This situation is particularly disturbing in light of our work with more than 600 Boston-area school leaders, which confirms what most know: The adults who work in schools carry with them extraordinary insights about schools and about improving schools. The issue, then, is not whether schoolpeople know much of value, but under what conditions they will reveal this rich knowledge of their craft so that it may become part of the discussion of school improvement. To be helpful, universities must engage in conversation with the people who live under the roof of the schoolhouse about the work that goes on there. Until dialogue replaces monologues, conversations between university and schoolpeople will have all of the resonance of one hand clapping.

Crossing Boundaries. A fourth roadblock to rich interaction between the worlds of school and university is that neither rewards those crossing the border between them very much. Few professors ever work in public schools and few schoolpeople ever work in higher education. Curiously, the education profession has made membership in its two major wings all but mutually exclusive. A citizen in one is suspect in the other. I even occasionally find that one who tries to be a citizen in both can be suspect in both.

If crossing boundaries is not rewarded by the host culture, neither is it rewarded by one's own culture. Academics are not promoted for talking to PTAs or consulting with classroom teachers. First-class citizenship and its institutional rewards come more from reading, writing, scholarly research, and distinguished teaching than from community service. And few teachers and school administrators are rewarded by their systems with release time or recognition for entering universities where they might study and reflect. Indeed, as we have seen, in many school cultures, to reveal oneself as an adult learner is considered both self-indulgent and an admission of deficiency. First-class citizenship in schools comes not from evidence of adult learning, but from learning on the part of students and satisfaction on the part of parents and supervisors.

How can schoolpeople find recognition within their systems for engaging in university activities? And how can university people gain greater recognition from their institutions for direct work with schools? Until the institutional reward systems begin to recognize the importance of participation in the world of the other, relationships between university and school will be limited by a kind of tourist-visa mentality. And as we know, there is only so much one can see and do as a tourist.

Theory Versus Practice. Yet another obstacle to close engagement between universities and schools has to do with the locus of theory and the locus of practice. The common rhetoric says, "Theory resides in universities and practice resides in schools." I find this conception simplistic and disturbing. It interferes with relations between school and university.

I know of no schoolteacher or principal who does not work from some organizing principle or framework—or, in university language, from a theory. Theories about teaching, parent involvement, curriculum improvement, and motivation abound in schools. Indeed they are the source of much discussion and tension among teachers, principals, and parents. Some of these school-based theories are good, some fragmentary, some implacable, and a few elegant. Be that as it may, school "practitioners" are theory makers as well as theory consumers. Conversely, most of my Harvard colleagues are practitioners. Most run and do things as well as think things. Academics run schools of education, departments, committees, and research projects. Most also practice as classroom teachers. A professor is no less a practitioner than a public school teacher. Some university people are good practitioners, some bad, some modest, many immodest, and a few elegant.

To suggest that theory is the province of the university as practice is of the schools sets up a caste system that, by anointing some of us, insults all of us. It is as if we are attributing to the other side fluency in a language we find foreign, when in fact we all speak a great deal of a common language. The question is how to remove schoolpeople and academics from the typecasting that so severely limits and strains our work together.

Contributions Universities Can Make

Drawing on my experience wading in the muddy waters at the intersection, I would like to offer some suggestions for making the relationship between school and university more fruitful.

The Need for Useful Research. There is useful and useless research; good and bad scholarship. Good academic scholarship and research about schools and improving schools should always be taken seriously by teachers and principals and parents. Rutter and others' *Fifteen Thousand Hours* (1979), Goodlad's *A Place Called School* (1984), and Sizer's *Horace's Compromise* (1984) have much to offer the school and university communities. But it is a mistake, I think, to take too seriously the capacity of educational research to directly improve schools. Academics have far greater success reaching other academics than they will probably ever have directly touching schoolpeople. Let me offer an illustration.

A few years ago, I spent an afternoon with twenty school educators from the Midwest. Eventually, we got on the subject of research. I asked these principals and teachers how they would respond to a widely publicized research study that supported school practices different from ones currently in use in their schools. "For instance," I elaborated, "who would do what differently because of the five characteristics of effective schools that Ronald Edmonds (1979) articulated so clearly?" My question generated some remarkable reactions:

"I don't look at the research. If you're oblivious to it, you never get yourself in the bind of having to reconcile its findings with your practice," said one administrator.

Another said, "You look at who's reporting the research—and then you kill the messenger. For example, Ron Edmonds never worked as a teacher or as a principal. Therefore, why should I take what he has to say about schools seriously?"

A third suggested, "Criticize the process that inflicts the research on you. If the superintendent tells you to implement an Edmonds-style school improvement project, but neither you nor other principals or teachers were involved in selecting that particular plan, then you reject Edmonds on that basis."

A principal who had just received her doctorate said that she would challenge the research methodology. "Edmonds drew his conclusions from a small sample of elementary schools. That's not statistically significant, so you can discount the work."

A teacher said he would "find a research study that contradicts the one I'm being asked to implement, one that supports my current practice. For every study favoring ability grouping, for instance, I can find one that shows that students do better in heterogeneous groups."

Another would "acknowledge the value of the research but declare it inappropriate in my setting." The speaker explained, "I'm a secondary school teacher in a suburban district. Edmonds did his work in urban elementary schools. You can't generalize from one type of school to the other."

The response of another school leader was to "selectively attend to the study—that is, pick out those pieces that confirm my current practice and ignore the rest. Research is a smorgasbord. You choose what you want and leave the rest."

Finally, one principal suggested, "Pay lip service to the research. Don't fight it. Say you are doing it; then they'll get off your back, and you can go on doing what you have been doing all along."

That conversation reverberates in my mind, and I continue to be troubled by it. Schoolpeople develop elaborate defenses with which to deflect new ideas imposed from outside. We educators seem to be gifted and talented at finding reasons why practices that have proven effective in other places cannot possibly be applied to our own school settings.

The variety and strength of these defense mechanisms are impressive—or depressing, depending on how you look at them. Clearly, these responses say a great deal about the likelihood of our making use of outside ideas and knowledge to improve the schools. It is striking, for instance, that during this two-hour conversation, not one of these educators suggested changing his or her behavior to comply more closely with the research findings or even to sift through the findings in order to use what might help—in other words, to make actions more congruent with the knowledge base offered by research.

The reactions of these twenty educators to research say a good deal about the limited capacity of the research community to directly influence the schools and of practitioners to make appropriate use of outside ideas. Most researchers, I think, work under the assumption that practitioners will welcome and accept new knowledge and put it to some kind of use in the field. The authors of the recent wave of national reports on school reform, for instance, seem to write with some expectation, if not confidence, that those who work in or are responsible for a school will select their study above all others and seek to bring the school into closer compliance with its recommendations. My conversation with these teachers and principals causes me to be more cautious.

This example notwithstanding, I think it important for higher educators to convey their work to audiences in the schools, through journals, books, lectures, consulting. Some *will* take from the smorgasbord. And all of this university thinking will continue to challenge, if not unsettle, the status quo in the schools.

I feel that a more promising means for academics to contribute to the improvement of our nation's schools is by helping school teachers and principals to clarify and to reveal their *own* rich thinking about good schools. Making craft knowledge visible dignifies and benefits the individual, other schoolpeople, and schools. Making practitioners' craft knowledge more widely visible also presents to audiences in academia a smorgasbord of insights that can challenge, if not unsettle, the status quo that is no less embedded in higher education than in schools. Some academics *will* take from the smorgasbord.

Halfway Houses. I see a pronounced need for agencies that can mediate between the cultures of school and university. The Principals' Center at Harvard is an example of a kind of "Trojan Horse" that has been wheeled inside the walled gates of the city. Out of it have sprung 600 real live school principals whose abundant presence and thinking and writing in libraries, classrooms, elevators, and dining areas has become undeniably visible. Conversely, the Center includes several Harvard faculty members each year on the program-planning board, as presenters at workshops, and in the Center administration. The Center, then, serves as a kind of "intercultural halfway house," permitting and encouraging schoolpeople to become first-class citizens in the university world. At the same time, it makes it convenient for faculty members to enter the world of school leaders.

As successful as these efforts may have been, the need for more substantial exchanges remains. More schoolpeople need to not only inhabit the university but to be engaged actively there as teachers and researchers. And academics need to not only associate frequently with schoolpeople but to assume for a period the job of teacher or administrator or some other kind of residency in the schools. The experience of the few who have risked citizenship in the schools suggests that not only do both worlds derive lasting benefits, but that it is possible for school and university to become part of the same world.

Writing. When we were first encouraging Boston-area principals to pay an annual membership fee, I was frequently confronted, in many languages, by the sometimes hostile question: "What has Harvard got to offer me that might be worth it?" A good question, carrying bad baggage, reminded us that the most pressing problems facing teachers and principals— difficult parents, poor discipline of students, low morale, severe budget cuts—are problems university professors probably know less about than do schoolpeople.

One promising response to the question was "writing." Perhaps not a welcome response, but promising. In academia, writing is the coin of the realm. Universities live and die by

it. Writing is generated, edited, discussed, critiqued, published, and celebrated. Reputations are built and promotions
are denied based on it. Those in universities may not know
much about classroom discipline, but they know a great deal
about the written word and its relation to clear thinking.
And clear thinking bears a close relationship to improved
practice.

I suggested in the previous chapter that writing about
school practice offers considerable rewards for practitioner,
author, and reader alike, and that writing can make a valuable contribution to improving schools. But few of the
nation's teachers and principals write about their important
work. What can universities do about that? Responses must
address and attempt to remedy the kinds of impediments cited
earlier: lack of time, the overwhelming complexity of the
subject, the terror of writing, the problem of generalizing,
interpersonal and political problems, and the legal problems
associated with publication.

Often what practitioners lack in order to set pen to
paper is the "handle" for a book project or an article—something distinct about teaching or administering that can provide the occasion for writing. Universities can be helpful here,
since professors are good at finding conceptual frameworks
in a confusion of data.

Another commodity the university has that school practitioners need is a "protected setting." One reason higher
educators write is that they live in an environment that values
writing, encouraging and rewarding it. The presence of a
library, colleagues who regularly read and criticize one another's papers, and a distance from the hurly-burly distractions
of the "real world" are all conditions conducive to writing.
Universities can insulate practitioners, for a while, from the
interpersonal and political problems that accompany writing
about their schools by offering a sanctuary.

Some principals' centers in universities commission
school practitioners to write case studies or prepare manuscripts on specific topics, such as "Ways of Encouraging Creativity in the Classroom" or "Teachers' Uses of Reward and

Punishment." Designation of the focus and assurance in advance of "acceptance" of the manuscript, coupled with the dignity and legitimization that comes with an honorarium, encourages many who might not otherwise consider writing about schools. I suspect a larger number of manuscripts might be generated in this way, which would be valuable in university courses and research projects. Assembling a library of the best of these practitioner accounts helps to diminish the distance between "theory" and "practice" that so divides the university and the school cultures.

Another promising way of assisting and encouraging schoolpeople to write is a deliberate pairing of a university researcher with a school practitioner as coauthors, sharing the responsibilities of writing with the professional rewards and satisfactions. I suspect that any school practitioner and any researcher would be able to find complementary skills and a common ground for cooperation. For example, I know of a principal now presiding over the closing of her school—an important and current issue these days. She has formed a partnership with a university researcher examining this question. The researcher gains from access to data and insight that only an "insider" can provide. The school's principal and teachers receive assistance from the researcher in the form of familiarity with the literature of school closings and skills in analysis that help them deal with this difficult issue. And with the assistance of a university person, principal and teachers become more confident about what to write and how to transform raw experience into prose. Once the pump has been primed, many practitioners continue to write about school closings or other issues without the assistance of the university partner. In short, higher educators, more comfortable and capable as researchers and authors, can help convey some of these qualities to elementary and secondary educators. The key here is a relationship not of subordinate to superordinate, but rather of parity and first-class citizenship for each party.

One reason school practitioners seldom write for publication is that they are unfamiliar with the sometimes obscure process of having manuscripts considered and accepted for publication. Where does one submit a manuscript? In what form? What appears to be a mysterious process shrouded with unknown protocol, coupled with a fear of rejection, often curtails tentative exploration. A university can provide a valuable service by helping edit and then broker manuscripts of practitioners to appropriate publications, as many university faculty do for their graduate students.

These are a few of the ways in which university members might assist school teachers and principals to make what they see and do more visible. There is ample room for a wider repertoire.

Certification. Another idea at the intersection of the domains of school and university that merits attention is *certification.* Teachers and principals aspiring for certification in most states usually fulfill requirements by taking courses at universities. This captive audience of prospective schoolpeople affords higher education a striking opportunity to lay the foundation for an enduring, helpful relationship, devoid of "bad baggage." Unfortunately, too often these opportunities are lost. Studies of very successful practitioners continue to reveal that most regard university course work as the least valuable component of their preparation.

Universities have a role to play in responsibly complying with certification responsibilities. They have an even more important role to play in the revision of dreary certification requirements and the creation of more inventive and promising ones. A definition of *professor* that, I have heard, originated in medieval German universities is "one who thinks otherwise." We need to "think otherwise" about certification.

I find that many certification plans offer a logical, coherent sequence that leads prospective teachers and principals from formal academic training through internship to certification. But often they are too ambitious. Impressive lists of regulations cannot be learned in any real sense in a lifetime, let alone in a couple of years. After the exam and certification some will know a little of the material; a few will know a lot of it; most will have "covered" it and forgotten it several months later. One must select a few of the most important and timely topics, and then make a serious attempt to help candidates learn skills in these critical areas. In order to make choices, criteria are needed. To the extent that a coherent vision exists for a desirable classroom and school, it is possible to narrow the lesson plan to a realistic focus.

I also question the common sequence of events in the certification curriculum. There is nothing in the literature of adult development that suggests that abstract book learning, followed by an internship experience in the schools, is a good formulation. To the contrary, most adults seem to learn better from a sequence of practice followed by a period of reflection, reading, and writing. Or, better still, by the juxtaposition of practice and reflection. The promising new curriculum at the Harvard Medical School, for instance, places aspiring physicians in a small group where they are immediately confronted with real clinical cases and medical problems. They learn to cooperate in diagnosing the malady and in deciding who will read and share what about the subject that might be helpful to the group in successfully diagnosing and treating the patient. They also learn a great deal about collegiality.

A good certification program fills schools with people who resemble the really distinguished teachers and principals we know. Why then don't we examine the prior experiences of a number of these unusual individuals to see how they came to be the way they are? My guess is that few got that way through conventional university course work or certification programs. What *were* the influential pieces of their experiences that certification programs might provide for others?

The most important piece for me in any curriculum intending to prepare professionals in education is the central place of lifelong learning. There is far more to know than time or energy to know it during a training experience. The field of education is changing as rapidly as other fields, such as health care. Every school and every problem and every context is different. Therefore, the bottom line for any period of induction into a profession must be to instill in each professional an inner resolve and capability to sustain learning on one's own initiative throughout one's career. This is the critical moment to create the foundation of a community of learners. A successful training curriculum prepares practitioners who will ask their own questions in their work and collaborate with colleagues in addressing them without depending on others outside the school. I have suggested that a central problem and paradox for public school educators is that we adults try to instill life and excitement and meaning into students' learning while we ourselves are dead as learners. I see attention in certification curricula devoted to teaching skills, to sound leadership, to supervised practice, and to instruction. Where is recognition of the crucial place of principals and teachers as head learners, as colleagues in learning? What in the selection, the curriculum, and certification values this quality, looks for it, attempts to measure its presence or absence, and aims to ensure that certification will mark the beginning, not the end, of the professional as learner?

I would like to see universities consider some other ideas as they seek to help improve schools.

Continuous Integration of Roles. Many agencies across the country provide professional development for aspiring and practicing teachers and school leaders. State departments of education, university departments, school districts, principals' centers, teachers' centers, assessment centers, and LEAD projects are all engaged in this important work. All believe that schools can be improved if leadership and teaching can be improved.

However, just as conditions within schools often inhibit the free and helpful exchange of ideas among teachers, parents, principals, and central office staff, so conditions within the profession discourage collegial conversation among the different providers of preservice and inservice education. When these groups do associate they are as likely to be competitors as colleagues. Universities can provide leadership for bringing these different organizations, and their often quite different worldviews, into closer physical and intellectual proximity where the larger picture may be assembled from the constituent parts.

A tremendous knowledge base about what works and what does not lies concealed in the work of the different providers of professional development for schoolpeople. These activities display wonderful variability. Each effort probably has a characteristic framework, a set of more or less coherent assumptions and principles about adult learning and its relationship to school improvement. Each holds a different set of beliefs about what successful school teachers and principals should know and be able to do, and an implicit distinguishing logic about how best to get them to be like that. These underlying beliefs and assumptions have a major influence on program, on evaluation, and on the experience of participants. Yet in few cases have providers explicitly clarified within their organization, let alone for the benefit of others, just what beliefs underlie practice. Universities seem to be in the strongest position to address this important task.

The Relationship of Teachers to Principals to Superintendents as Educational Leaders. I will argue in the next chapter that school leadership is not specific to the role of "principal," although this individual is frequently considered the most visible and important school leader. If schools are to improve from within, leadership must emanate from many sources in interaction, including teachers, principals, parents, and students. The concept of shared leadership and of a school as a *community of leaders* whose very mission is to help enlist all members of the community to make important contributions to the work of the school would enrich and refresh role-bound training programs. This implies that university departments, such as teacher education and educational administration, must begin to emerge from *their* "separate caves" and work to build bridges between school roles such as that of "teacher" and "principal" with the expectation that these bridges will endure when the new teachers and principals take their places in the schools. Fundamental school improvement will not come from teacher training for some and administrator training for others; it will come, I believe, from leadership preparation and interdependence for all.

The Relationship of Preservice and Inservice Training. Within state departments of education and universities, it is common for certain persons to be responsible for the preparations of aspiring teachers, principals, and superintendents, while others—frequently in a different location—provide professional development for practicing school personnel. Seldom do these two worlds converge. Yet many promising examples from teacher and leadership training organizations suggest that when preservice and inservice are linked, everyone benefits. For instance, at many principals' centers experienced principals run seminars and provide other activities for aspiring principals. The research on adult development suggests that adults in their forties and fifties experience a need to mentor, to assist those who aspire to the positions they hold. Conversely, teachers and principals-in-training often report that they learn as much about the positions to which they aspire from those who currently occupy them as from university course work. Each domain has much to gain from and contribute to the other.

Continuous Relationship of Practitioners and Providers. All over the country the preparation of school personnel is being revised as legislative committees, state department officials, and professors debate questions of training, selection, and inservice. But seldom does information that would inform questions of policy, program, and pedagogy flow from the consumers of these experiences—those who have *been* certified—to providers. Seldom do successful teachers and administrators sit at the table where important decisions are being made about how to train, select, and sustain successful teachers and principals. The insights and feedback from consumers must be continuously tapped by providers if these programs are to improve.

What Has Constituted and What Does and Might Constitute Staff Development? The history of training reform often leads to a search for new patches for leaky tires. But many of the problems of training are of a conceptual nature: the separation of course work from internships and practice, mandatory attendance for pedestrian activities, a preoccupation with caution. We need to continuously juxtapose improving what is with a consideration and a creation of what might be. Many examples of inventive thinking about adult development abound. One has only to look to Outward Bound, IBM, the theatre, medicine. We in education need to search for new visions of schools, of teaching, and of leadership in schools, and at the same time devise equally revolutionary conceptions of adult development.

Recognition and Respectability. My work in schools and in universities suggests that perhaps the most influential contribution a university can make in assisting teachers, parents, and principals in improving their schools is to convey prestige and respectability to them. Universities are in a unique position to bestow recognition on schoolpeople whose lives are so badly devoid of it. Those in higher education can legitimize the efforts of schoolpeople and convey in a thousand ways that what goes on in schools is important, that those who work in schools are important, and that their writing and their craft knowledge are important to school and university alike. The academic community values large-scale, university-based research. But useful knowledge about schools can come as well from the identification of good practice, the codification of good practice, and attempts to communicate good practice. When university people come to recognize that the thinking and writing of teachers and principals can also be characterized by internal rigor, even elegance, they will indeed be in a position to help. This calls on higher educators to subordinate or redirect their own needs for authority and recognition to some extent. The outcome for schools may be worth the exchange.

There are many ways the imprimatur of the university

can be imparted to those in the schools. At one school where I was principal, we devised a contract with Brandeis University to cooperate in its undergraduate teacher certification program. About a dozen students were placed with as many of our teachers. Each year a group of teachers ran what were called "Brandeis seminars," which helped the student teachers learn instructional methodology. Teachers enlisted fellow teachers as faculty. Topics included discipline, observing children, record keeping, curriculum, and getting a teaching job. Mutual visibility and exchange of craft knowledge abounded.

Teachers were modestly paid to share their knowledge with the prospective teachers. More important, they became, in a real sense, university faculty. These opportunities conveyed several important messages: "We are aware of the many good things you are doing; we value these things; we believe others would benefit from knowing what you are thinking and doing; we believe strongly enough about this and value your expertise enough that we will convene the student teachers and pay you." These messages, so seldom communicated to teachers, affirm importance, dignity, and professionalism. When teachers receive this kind of recognition, they go to extraordinary lengths to justify it. They reflect on their practice, translating intuitive behavior into more conscious, visible information that can be useful to others. This process results in extraordinary learning and classroom improvement for teachers and for students of teaching alike.

Recognition these days is the commodity in greatest supply in universities and in shortest supply to teachers and principals. It should not be difficult to find other ways of turning this imbalance into opportunities for closer school-university collaboration—and into opportunities for improving schools. There is a prevailing notion in many central offices, in state departments of education, and in universities that schools are not capable of improving themselves. This belief has led to a long history of outside prescriptions, many of which are currently before the nation for consideration. Rather than trying to draw up lists and offer prescriptions for how students, teachers, and principals should behave—

a tack that offers only illusive and illusionary control and change—there may be another, no less illusive, but more promising tack. Educators outside the schools can search out and provide conditions that will make the improvement of schools likely by those who reside within them.

I am uncertain, even after these many years, whether the Principals' Center is a pearl or a grain of sand in the Harvard oyster. Nor am I sure whether a polish or an irritant is the better metaphor for interaction between school and university. But I am sure that it is vital to the life of both school and university to confront the many sources of dissonance between us, to acknowledge the many opportunities that now present themselves, and to think freshly about our relationship if, together, we are to strengthen the schools. I am confident that school and university can become members of the same community of learners and leaders.

TEN

Becoming a Community
of Leaders

A few months ago, I heard a teacher recite from memory an unusual and haunting piece of poetry a portion of which appears here (by permission):

> And one day, lying alone on the lawn on my back, hearing only the moan and groan of some far off train on a distant track, I saw above me, 2,000 feet or more, something which to this day, I must say, I've never seen anything like before. The head goose, the leader of the "V," suddenly swerved out, leaving a vacancy that promptly was filled by the bird behind. The leader then flew alongside, the formation growing wide, and took his place at the back of the line—and they never missed a beat! [Stomberg, 1982, p. 1].

In the piece, two important ideas emerge—leadership and community. It is not difficult to see an analogy between the geese and the schools, each implying a "community of leaders."

Like most of us, I have been reading some of the recent national reports on education. I find that the concept of shared school leadership has become both fashionable and controversial. It appears that concern about the relationship between teacher and principal, around schoolwide decision making, will be with us for a good while. I hope so.

Unfortunately, well-intentioned efforts to involve teachers in decision making have exacerbated tensions among teachers and between teachers and principals. Teachers and their associations have responded in a variety of ways—with anger that it has taken so long to include them, with suspicion that they are being tricked, and with confidence that the revolution is now at hand.

The national professional principals' associations have responded defensively to the idea that teachers might "lead" schools. So has the American Association of School Administrators, which issued a policy statement that cautiously "encourages schools and districts to establish formal procedures that will promote appropriate involvement of teachers in decision making." This would take place under the direction of a "strong, effective principal. Substituting a lead teacher or a committee of teachers for the principal is unacceptable" (Rodman, 1987, p. 9). Far from lead geese moving back from the head of the line to allow others a turn at leading, far from building collegiality, attempts to rearrange decision making within a school seem to be ruffling feathers.

For several years, thanks to mastery learning, the effective schools literature, and the concept of high expectations, most of us have been saying and seeing that "all children can learn." Initially, many teachers, principals, parents, and even children were skeptical. Now the belief that "all children can learn" is widespread and the implications for instruction and for students have become profound.

For some time now, principals' centers have based their work on the belief that "all principals can learn" and that "all principals can teach." Many were skeptical of these propositions. Yet the conviction that principals have substantial professional knowledge that is of immense value to others in improving schools and that they can convey these insights to their colleagues is having profound implications for principals, for their professional development, and for the improvement of their schools.

I would like to suggest another proposition: "All teachers can lead." Skeptics might say "a few teachers" or "some" or even "many." But there is an important part of the life and work of the entire school at which every teacher is good, wants to become good, and can become good. Teachers harbor extraordinary leadership capabilities, and their leadership is a major untapped resource for improving our nation's schools. All teachers can lead. The world will come to accept that all teachers can lead, as many now accept that "all children can learn" and "all principals can learn" if we can overcome the many impediments facing teachers and principals that block teachers' leading, and if we can find conditions under which teachers will exercise that leadership.

As principal, I used to think I shared leadership. I did. Or I should say I went as far as I could go or felt the school could go. But reflecting a decade later on my leadership, I see that I stopped well short of a community of leaders. Leadership for me was delegating, giving away, or sharing participation in important decisions to others so long as the curriculum, pupil achievement, staff development, and, of course, stability were not much altered. Now I see it differently. Rather, my vision for a school is a place whose very mission is to ensure that students, parents, teachers, and principals all become school leaders in some ways and at some times. Leadership is making the things happen that you believe in or envision. Everyone deserves a chance. Schools can help all adults and youngsters who reside there learn how to lead and enjoy the recognition, satisfaction, and influence that come from serving the common interest as well as one's self-interest.

I would like to consider the idea of a school as a community of leaders by examining what students, teachers, and principals might do there.

Students as Leaders

Students can be school leaders. When we think of student leadership, we usually think of elected student councils and other means by which students are encouraged to provide leadership for their class or their school. All too often, student councils become preoccupied with the senior prom or become a transparent attempt to co-opt students into the service of teachers' and administrators' goals. Seldom are they a forum in which students make what they believe in happen. Currently, much is being said about the value of "community service" for students, particularly for adolescents who harbor so much energy, idealism, and moral outrage. Academic credit is given for some high school students to work in hospitals, libraries, and nursery schools. As yet, few students and schools have turned the concept of community service to improving their *own* school community.

In an elementary school where I was principal during the open education/traditional education years, I remember having difficulty handling the number of visitors to classrooms. Our school had tried to develop classes that reflected each teacher's beliefs. There were no labels, no "open classroom" signs, and happily, only modest tension around classroom structure and philosophy. It was worth a visit to see desks in rows and workbooks in one classroom adjoined by reading lofts and gerbils in another—and the teachers working closely together.

We welcomed visitors from colleges, other schools, the central office, and prospective parents. Yet none of us had time to give tours, answer delicate questions, and mediate between teachers and visitors. We decided to turn for help to fifth- and sixth-grade youngsters who had expressed an interest in taking on this important schoolwide responsibility. Two teachers developed a "training program" that acquainted prospective student tour guides with every nook and cranny of the school, from the science labs upstairs to the boiler room in the basement. Students talked with each adult who worked in the school about what they were doing and how they would like to receive visitors. We helped students anticipate tough, hypothetical questions, such as, "How are students assigned to a classroom each year?" After a few weeks of this unusual catechism, a dozen students were ready. They had found access to parts of the school few knew existed. They had seen the whole building, its space, faculty, philosophy, and current problems—an opportunity available to few others.

When that first group of student teachers from Brandeis

arrived, the fifth and sixth graders were ready. Each youngster responded to the secretary's call by conducting an hour-long tour of the school for each student teacher. The college students and their supervisor were impressed. The college teachers were impressed. I was impressed. And most important, perhaps, the youngsters were impressed—by how much they knew about their school and by the responsibility with which they had been entrusted. Subsequent tours included school board members, the mayor, prospective parents, and even intrigued teachers within the school. The underlying questions in the minds of most visitors to most schools are, "I wonder how students like it here? What do they learn? What's this school really like?" The medium was the message. Now, ten years later, a visitor is still assisted in becoming familiar with the school by a student guide.

In all my work with students I have never known one to "blow it" when the chips were down. Whether they are faced with an important tour or a stage production, children rise to the occasion. Being entrusted with important school-wide responsibility brings forth leadership, maturity, and learning. Are there any more important hopes for the school experience than these? The example of student tour guides suggests that maybe "all children can lead." It also suggests the rich possibilities of a community of leaders in which students, as well as adults, can become first-class citizens.

Teachers as Leaders

Shortly after my arrival as principal of an elementary school, a veteran teacher sent me a memo indicating his intention to stay out of school until the "deplorable and illegal fire safety standards have been corrected." A challenge to the new authority? Perhaps. An unwelcome hassle from an unexpected quarter? Perhaps. And an opportunity. Perhaps.

In a long talk with the teacher, his concern for the safety of the children, his anger about the current situation, and his willingness to do something about it emerged. At the conclusion of the conversation, I asked him if he would accept responsibility for the fire standards of the entire school and assume the position of "fire marshal"—all of the responsibility. He was appropriately suspicious. The next day he agreed. I gave him the key to the fire alarm system and pledged my support for any plan he proposed. I asked that he talk with me from time to time as his plan developed. A risk—for both of us.

Somehow, in addition to his full-time teaching responsibilities, this teacher began to devise a most incredible school fire safety system. He met with each class and teacher and talked about the seriousness of fire in a four-story, fifty-year-old brick and wooden building full of papers and people. He held a separate fire drill for each class, established a route of exit, and assessed with teacher and students how the drill had gone, what could be improved, and how long it took to evacuate the building. Then he announced the first schoolwide fire drill. The fire chief from the city attended and watched in wonderment as 450 children and 30-some adults cleared the building quickly and quietly. Our "fire marshal" informed their "fire marshal" that he was concerned by how long it took *them* and their equipment to reach the school. He told them that once a year he would call a drill and time the officials to see how quickly they could respond!

Furthermore, he reasoned that in the event of a real fire during the long New England winter, the population of the school (many at work without shoes and coats) would have to stand in the snow and freezing cold for an indeterminate time. This was unacceptable. He visited a nearby church and made arrangements with the pastor to secure a key. During the next drill the entire school filed into predetermined pews of the church. I will never forget his solemn assessment of our performance from the altar.

Unusual lengths to go for safety? A pathological obsession about fires? Too much time spent off "the basics"? Most of us would rather have our own children in a school that took safety this seriously than the one that had been operating the previous year—or the school in which the principal tried to administer fire safety along with everything else.

When teachers are enlisted and empowered as school leaders, everyone can win. Other teachers' concerns are frequently better understood by one of their fellows than by someone who performs a different job. Important schoolwide issues receive more care and attention when the adult responsible is responsible for few other major areas. And the principal wins by recognizing that there is plenty of leadership to go around. If the principal tries to do all of it, much of it will be left undone by anyone. Leadership is not a zero-sum game in which one person gets some only when another loses some. In fact, the principal gains influence and demonstrates leadership by entrusting some of it to others. Being accorded leadership generates new leadership.

Additionally, important needs of the teacher-leader may be met. In this case, the teachers' rapport with the faculty improved. He was dubbed "Sparky" and, at an end-of-year faculty meeting, was awarded a shiny new red fireman's hat (the kind about which eight-year-old boys dream at Christmas) on which was emblazoned "Chief," recognition that he *was* chief—of something. Other teachers can become chief of something, too. And, if each of thirty teachers were to become chief of something, a school would be well along the path toward a community of leaders.

But many teachers and principals feel that teaching and leadership are mutually exclusive. One visitor to a school who was interested in leadership asked to "shadow" a teacher for a day. The teacher responded, stating, "I'm not a leader. I'm just a teacher. If you want to see leadership, go shadow the principal." To be a leader is to be an administrator. That all teachers lead within their classrooms does not seem to count. Leadership happens among adults. It is commonly held that if you are a teacher, the only way to become a leader is to leave teaching.

There may be few opportunities for teachers to offer schoolwide leadership. Others may not feel it possible. Yet for more teachers the question is, "Why would I want to lead anyway? Shut the door and leave me alone." As one principal put it, "Teachers in my building don't want more participation. Most teachers already feel overwhelmed and over-worked." Teachers spend vast quantities of time and energy beyond their work hours correcting papers, repairing what happened today, and preparing for what may happen tomorrow. An opportunity for leadership, like an opportunity for learning, is seen as an opportunity to deplete more time and energy. Opportunities for teachers to coordinate curricula, run meetings, and manage fire drills are peculiar opportunities, indeed. The would-be teacher-leader seeks fulfillment and satisfaction, but more often than not encounters committee work, meetings, and conflict. Already bombarded with interpersonal overload, few teachers are eager to accept such "opportunities."

When others are making the decisions, teachers can resist, lobby, hold out, and, in inventive ways, attempt to influence a situation to their own advantage. When teachers work for the common good, they give up a large measure of self-interest in the outcome. With leadership and responsibility comes the need to see others' points of view and act fairly in their eyes. Many teachers are not willing to make this trade.

And, as principals know, no decision pleases everyone. In fact, any decision displeases someone. Why would teachers want to engender the wrath of their fellows? "Let the principal do it. That is what the principal is paid for." And, given the distance in many places between union and management, why should a teacher do what an administrator is supposed to do, thereby lightening the load of the adversary and increasing one's own? As one teacher put it, "to go across can be debilitating."

The rewards of leadership, then—so treasured in the eyes of teachers—are often illusory, no more immediate and satisfying for teachers than for principals. For most teachers the school world is the world within the classroom. Teaching. Because "every teacher can lead" clearly does not mean that every teacher wants to lead, should lead, or should be expected or required to lead.

There is a touch of irony in the fact that those in history who have been most widely celebrated as "teachers" have also been leaders. Socrates, Plato, Jesus, Moses, Gandhi are all names synonymous with teaching and leading. But teacher leadership is clearly not a common contemporary condition. Why, then, did Sparky agree to serve as school fire marshal? Why, for that matter, would *any* teacher choose to engage in serious, sustained school leadership?

Public policymakers respond that opportunities for teachers to lead will attract more able people to the profession. And by engaging teachers in leadership activities, the very able, once empowered, ennobled, and challenged, will choose to remain in teaching. Others argue that leadership opportunities will bring out the best from teachers; and the very best from teachers will bring out the very best from their students. Teacher leadership will raise pupil achievement. For instance, *Time for Results: The Governors' 1991 Report on Education,* issued by the Center for Policy Research and Analysis of the National Governors' Association in 1986, proposes less regulation of teachers if they will provide leadership at the school level and accept responsibility for student achievement.

The literature of successful businesses, from Japanese hi-tech firms to IBM, offers evidence that when workers participate in decision making, both their satisfaction and the quality of their work rise. Teacher-leaders, too, it is reasoned, will become more invested in the school and in its success if they are stockholders. By sharing leadership, teachers will feel more ownership of and commitment to decisions. And by providing teachers with leadership opportunities, one accords them recognition. Therefore, they will work harder and better and longer. In short, research suggests that the greater the participation in decision making, the greater the productivity, job satisfaction, and organizational commitment.

That is why policymakers and businesspeople would have teachers lead. But, given the reasons "why not" suggested earlier, why would any *teacher* want a hand in major school decisions? One teacher put it this way:

What is the passion I have for education? The classroom experience. That is what I love. On reflecting upon it I realized that I love my own experience; that which occurs within the walls of my room and with students I call mine. What happens in my room, I like to think, is quality learning. What happens outside my room has very little to do with me. And that, quite simply, is what's wrong with public schools.

Another teacher put it differently: "The concept of teacher-leader ought not to be such a difficult one to adopt. After all, teachers are leaders in the classroom every day. There is no reason why the skills of the classroom cannot be transferred to areas of the school life outside the classroom." And another said:

Teachers are leaders every day in dozens of ways. We provide educational direction and create the kind of educational environments we believe in for our students. We work with other teachers to create new curricula or to consult on problems we have with students. We work with parents in reflecting on their children's development and by providing information about academic matters. We voice matters of concern for ourselves, our colleagues, our students and administrators, and frequently initiate major programmatic changes in our schools.

To assert one's leadership as a teacher, often against forces of administrative resistance, takes commitment to an educational ideal. It also requires the energy to combat one's own inertia caused by habit and overwork. And it requires a certain kind of courage to step outside of the small prescribed circle of traditional "teacher tasks," to declare through our actions that we care about and take responsibility for more than the minimum, more than what goes on within the four walls of our classrooms.

Many teachers feel, then, that no matter how fulfilling, how important, and how successful their work within classrooms may be, there is more to teaching. Some teachers become concerned about the whole school because they think "if only someone will . . ." When "someone doesn't" for long enough, they become the "someone." They are propelled from classroom to school leadership by anger:

> I've thought about my own development as a school leader; it was clearly anger which pushed me out on the leadership "limb." Put another way, anger provided the adrenaline which made it possible for me to take the risk of assuming a leadership role. Moreover, beyond the initial "push," anger fueled the courage to persist in a leadership role which was often uncomfortable, unpleasant and unfamiliar. For me then, anger both precipitated and sustained my role as a faculty leader. Anger enabled me to find my voice and compelled me to speak out publicly. Speaking publicly, in turn, required that I channel my anger into constructive and articulate criticisms of and challenges to my principal's policies and decisions.

And many teachers want to lead for precisely the reasons others do not. They derive respect, if not acclaim, from other teachers for their efforts; they derive energy from leadership activities that fuels, rather than depletes, their classroom activities; by leading, they find they can more fully understand the points of view of other teachers and administrators; they enjoy meetings and orchestrating interactions with other adults as well as with children; they find they learn by leading, that leadership offers profound possibilities for professional development; and they aspire to distinguish themselves with respect to their peers.

In short, opportunities to engage in school leadership are attractive for Sparky and other teachers because they offer possibilities for improving teaching conditions; they replace the solitary authority of the principal with a collective authority; they provide a constructive format in which adults can interact, thereby overcoming daily classroom isolation with youngsters; they help transform schools into contexts for adults' as well as children's learning; and participation in leadership builds community.

The Principal and a Community of Leaders

Principals, by virtue of the authority of their position, are seen as school leaders. Many principals attempt to exercise an authoritarian, hierarchical kind of leadership: They arrange schedules that mandate who is supposed to be where and doing what; they maintain tight control over money supplies and behavior; they dictate curriculum, goals, and means. An inevitable consequence of this patriarchal model of leadership—aside from a certain amount of order and productivity—is the creation of a dependent relationship between principal and teacher. Furthermore, many tasks in schools, such as helping disturbed children, coordinating curriculum, and evaluating pupils, are too complex and frightening for any one person to deal with. Consequently, the model of the principal who unilaterally "runs" a school no longer works very well.

Successful principals, like successful college presidents these days, are successful less as charismatic authority figures than as coalition builders. The increasing specialization of teachers, for instance, signals that the principal can no longer be the master teacher well versed in instructing handicapped children, students who are gifted and talented, beginning reading, and advanced math. Hence, it has become increasingly important to share leadership and to no longer even aspire to fully understand and control every aspect of the school.

Recently I participated in a lengthy conversation about shared leadership with an elementary school principal and a junior high school teacher. We agreed on several assumptions about teachers as leaders: All teachers have leadership tendencies; schools badly need teachers' leadership; teachers badly need to exercise that leadership; teachers' leadership has not been forthcoming; the principal has been at the center of both successes and failures of teachers' leadership; and principals who are most successful as leaders themselves are somehow able to enlist teachers in providing leadership for the entire school.

What, then, can principals do to develop a community of leaders within a school? What do principals do that thwarts the development of teacher leadership? What do principals do that makes the emergence of school leadership from teachers more likely?

Articulating the Goal. In order to move a school from where it is to where one's vision would have it be, it is necessary to convey what the vision is. As we will see in the following chapter, this is risky. Many principals may not be sure of what their vision is. They may not want to face the faculty and parental dissonance that might surface if they shared their vision. They may not want to expose their thinking to the central office, which may not see the connection between, say, "a community of leaders" and minimum competence in three-place multiplication. Consequently, few administrators telegraph their vision to the school community, preferring to believe that "they'll figure it out." A community of leaders and the involvement of teachers, students, and parents in school leadership is more likely to occur when the principal openly articulates this goal in meetings, conversations, newsletters, faculty memos, and community meetings. In this way shared leadership becomes part of the school culture.

Relinquishing Authority to Teachers. As we have seen, there are short lists and long lists of behaviors of "effective principals." They include continuous monitoring of performance, exercising strong leadership, and involving parents. I have never seen the "ability to relinquish" on such a list. Many principals feel they have too little authority over a tottering building. To convey any authority to others is illogical. It is against human nature for us to relinquish power when we will probably be held accountable for what others do with it. One should accumulate and consolidate, not relinquish. This leads to the common belief that "I cannot leave my building." A most important item in any list of characteristics of effective principals is the capacity to relinquish, because only then can the latent, creative powers of teachers be released.

It is important for a principal to relinquish decision-making authority to teachers. But teachers will not become leaders in the school community if, when the going gets tough and the angry phone calls come from the central office, the principal violates the trust and reasserts authority over the issues. It takes only one or two incidents where the rug is pulled from beneath teachers' leadership before teachers secede from the community of leaders. The principal must bet on a horse and have the courage and trust to stick with it and help it finish. To change the bet in the middle of the race is to create conditions under which everyone loses.

Involving Teachers Before Decisions Are Made. It is common in the world of teachers and principals for a problem, like inadequate fire safety, to emerge, and for the principal to quickly reach a solution (bringing in the fire chief to lecture students and teachers) and then invite a teacher to "handle" the situation. This is an opportunity for maintenance, not leadership, which few teachers will embrace. The energy, the fun, the commitment around leadership comes from brainstorming one's *own* solutions and then trying to implement them. For a community of leaders to develop, tough important problems need to be conveyed to teachers before, not after, the principal has played them out.

Which Responsibility Goes to Whom? Wanting desperately to resolve a problem, the principal often selects a responsible, trusted teacher who has successfully handled similar challenges. But, by relying on the tried and proven teacher, the principal rewards competence with additional hard work. The tried teacher is a tired teacher. It will be only a matter of time before the overburdened teacher burns out and leaves teaching or leaves the school, concluding that if one is going to *act* like an assistant principal, one might as well be *paid* like an assistant principal. Other often-chosen teachers will one day declare, "I'm drowning and I must return my attentions to the classroom. I'm sorry, but I can't do it."

The better match, as in Sparky's case, may be between an important school issue and a teacher who feels passionately about that issue. For one teacher, it is fire safety; for another, the supply closet; while another would favor reforming the science curriculum, finding both fire safety and the supply closet menial tasks, not leadership opportunities. Teacher leadership is less a question of according trusted teachers responsibility for important issues than of ensuring that all teachers are given ownership for a responsibility about which they care deeply. One person's junk is another person's treasure.

Reliance on a few proven teachers for schoolwide leadership also excludes the majority of untried teachers from the community of leaders, contributing to divisiveness and developing little of a community. For Sparky, the opportunity to have the "key" had far more meaning than for other teachers who had been offered and accepted many keys. His inclusion expanded the community by one.

Too often the criterion for bestowal of the "key" of leadership is evidence that a person knows how to do it. Yet the innovative solutions come more often from teachers who do not know how to do it but want to learn how. This is where leadership and staff development intersect. The moment of greatest learning for any of us is when we find ourselves responsible for a problem that we care desperately to resolve. Then we need and seek out assistance. We are ready to learn. At this moment, the principal (and faculty) have a responsibility and an opportunity to assist the teacher in developing leadership skills and finding success with responsibility. Mere delegation or "being kept informed" is not sufficient involvement on the principal's part for the development of a community of leaders. Unsuccessful leaders do not make a community of leaders. Most teachers, like most principals, need assistance in becoming successful school leaders. The principal who supports and teaches the "beginning school leader" assumes a burden of considerable risk, time, and patience. "It would be safer, easier, and quicker to handle it myself." Yet this is what is really meant by shared leadership." It is interactive, interdependent. Communities of leaders beget communities of learners.

By turning for leadership to untried and perhaps untrusted teachers who express a passionate interest in an issue, as Sparky did, everyone can win. The overburdened teacher receives no further burden; the teacher who displays excitement or anger about an issue is enlisted in the growing community of leaders. The teacher comes alive as an adult learner as well as a leader. And I think the principal wins. If the principal can help anoint and support the initial efforts of teacher-leaders this year, those efforts will be rewarded next year by a level of independence when much less will be needed from the principal.

Shared Responsibility for Failure. If the principal conveys responsibility to a teacher for an important schoolwide issue and the teacher stumbles, the principal has several options. Blame the teacher. "I entrusted leadership and authority for fire safety to Sparky and he blew it. Now I'll find someone more trustworthy who can do it better or I'll do it myself." This may protect the principal in the short run, but in the long run neither Sparky nor other teachers will choose to play again. Without the provision of a safety net by the principal, few teachers will aspire to walk the high wire— no community of leaders. Or the principal can become the lone lightning rod. "I am captain of the ship; it has gone aground. I assume responsibility." A needlessly lonely and self-punitive position.

If the principal bets on this horse and it runs poorly, "we" are responsible, for together we have given our best efforts. Both have wrestled with something of importance to them and to the school that bonds them. Responsibility for failure is shared. Usually the world of schools deals more kindly with mistakes made by a coalition of teacher and administrator than when either errs alone. The important question to ask is not "Whose fault is it?", but "What happened, what can we learn from it, and how might we do it better next time?" The principal and teacher who share leadership have hope for developing collegiality, staff development, and morale. There is much to be gained, then, by both teacher and principal from failing together.

   Teachers Take Credit for Success. Whereas it is important to the development of a community of leaders that failures be shared by teacher and principal, I think it equally important that success reflect on the teacher, not the principal. The principal has many visible occasions during the school day and year to be the "hero": running the assembly, coming in over the loudspeaker, sending the notice to parents, meeting with the press about the National Merit Finalists. For the teacher, there are precious few opportunities to experience and enjoy recognition from the school community. For the principal to hog or share the limelight is to reduce the meaning and the recognition for the teacher and make less likely continuation of membership in the community of leaders.

   Visible, schoolwide success replenishes the teacher personally and professionally. I have seen classroom performance, morale, commitment to teaching, and relationships with colleagues all benefit from public recognition. Additionally, teachers should enjoy the success because they have done most of the work. My part in the fire safety plan occupied a fraction of the time Sparky put in. Mine were prime minutes, perhaps, but there were few of them.

   Principals, of course, have their own needs for success and recognition that often impede the development of a community of leaders. But, in the long run, teacher success begets further teacher leadership and success. The school improves. And the principal comes in for ample credit as "the one who pulled it off." Everyone wins.

All Teachers Can Lead. Just as high expectations that "all children can learn" have been associated with unexpected learning on the part of children whose background might not predict such achievement, high expectations on the part of principals and others that all teachers can be responsible, committed school leaders make more likely the emergence of leadership tendencies that all teachers possess.

How might principals' expectations for teachers as leaders be raised and conveyed? Principals can articulate a community of leaders as a goal, ask teachers to think about a piece of the school for which each would like responsibility, and then look for and celebrate examples of teacher leadership when they emerge.

"I Don't Know How." The foregoing discussion about principals helping induct teachers as citizens of a community of leaders implies that the principal knows how to do something, but, for a variety of reasons, would prefer that the teacher do it. I probably could have handled the problem of fire safety, although not as well as Sparky. Yet principals who always know how to do something perpetuate that "burden of presumed competence." A principal is hired from among 100 candidates because the selection committee supposes he or she knows how to do it. Therefore, for principals to admit that they do not know how is a sign of weakness, at best, and incompetence at worst. As we have seen, many principals succumb to the burden of presumed competence by pretending, and sometimes even *convincing* themselves, that they know how. This can kill the development of a community of leaders. The invitation for a teacher to take on fire safety may often be framed, then, as a veiled challenge to see if the teacher can do it as well as the principal. Competition on the part of the teacher to exceed the principal's knowledge and skills in turn may engender a wish on the part of the principal that the teacher fail. In such a case, school leadership becomes an occasion to renew adversarial relationships all too latent among teachers and principals.

Teachers know that principals do not know how to do it all. Surprising results are achieved when a principal initiates conversations with a teacher by announcing honestly, "I've never set up a fire safety system before. I've got some ideas, but I don't know how." *I don't know how.* This declaration by the principal becomes a powerful invitation to teachers. It suggests that the principal and school need help, and that the teacher can provide the help. And it gives the teacher room to risk not knowing how either and perhaps to fail. More likely, the teacher can emerge a genuinely helpful leader of the school and friend and colleague of the principal. *I don't know how* is an attractive, disarming, and realistic invitation likely to be accepted and handled with responsibility—and with collegiality.

Personal Security. These suggestions for teacher and principal to move a school toward a community of leaders imply a level of personal security on the part of principal as well as teacher. To publicly articulate a personal vision, relinquish control, empower and entrust teachers, involve teachers early, accord responsibility to untried teacher-leaders, share responsibility for teacher failure, accord responsibility to teachers for success, and have confidence that all teachers can lead, principals have to be psychologically secure individuals who are willing to take risks. The principals' personal security is a precondition on which development of communities of leaders rests. With some measure of security on the part of principals these ideas have plausibility; without security they have little. Yet, as I have suggested earlier, there are many forces at work that give principals good reason to feel insecure. Who will supply *their* safety net?

The security of principals might be strengthened in several ways. During the preservice preparation of aspiring principals, including certification requirements, university course work, and peer interaction, the concept of shared leadership can be introduced and legitimized, so that candidates might become familiar and comfortable with the idea of teachers as colleagues in leadership.

During the process to select a new principal, criteria are put forth and decisions made on the basis of a host of factors usually determined within the school district. Seldom is "personal security" among them. Yet interview techniques and other oral and written instruments exist that might help identify this important quality.

A third promising point of possible influence on principals' security occurs at the *inservice* level. Principals have as a context the school over which they preside, a sense of the faculty's and of the student body's differences and strengths, and teachers and fellow principals with whom to explore the unfamiliar, perhaps threatening idea of shared leadership.

But, as we have seen, schools are organizations that suffer from scarce resources and recognition. Teachers compete with teachers; principals compete with principals; and teachers compete with principals for these precious commodities. For principals to feel sufficiently secure and in control in order to share authority with others, their own needs for recognition, success, and safety must be acknowledged and addressed.

The Program Advisory Board at the Principals' Center at Harvard recently selected shared leadership as a focus for one semester in the belief that "shared leadership expands the possibilities for school improvement, increases commitment, complicates decision-making, and makes for more effective education for children" (Graduate School of Education, Harvard University, 1987). Two-hour workshops with titles such as "Building School Coalitions"; "A Nation Prepared: Teachers for the 21st Century"; "The Principal and the Conditions of Teaching"; "A Case for Shared Leadership"; "The Revolution That Is Overdue"; "Who Owns the Curriculum?"; "School Improvement Councils"; and "Working Together for Quality Education" occupied the attention of many principals as well as teachers. These discussions may not have transformed the insecure into the secure, but they have made the concept of school as a community of leaders more compelling and less risky.

Communities of Leaders. The vision of a school as a community of leaders is not a fantasy. When the National Education Association (NEA) was founded in 1870, its membership included not only teachers but many teacher-educators, principals, and superintendents, all banded together in the cause of good schools.

A century later, the NEA—now a teachers' organization—has joined with the National Association of Secondary School Principals to create *Ventures in Good Schooling* (1986), a project that seeks collaborative schools in which the professional autonomy of teachers and managerial authority of principals are harnessed. Among the recommendations of this effort are that principals involve faculty members in decision making; that teachers participate in the school budgeting process and in evaluating principals' performance; that principals seek teachers' advice on staffing needs and decisions; and that principals and teachers jointly devise a schoolwide plan for instructional improvement and for recognizing student achievement. This is but one promising step toward a community of leaders.

Several secondary schools, including the Cambridge School of Weston and Brookline and Andover High Schools in Massachusetts and Hanover High School in New Hampshire, have been working to create what they call "democratic schools." A town meeting form of school government provides teachers and students a structure for participating in the major decisions confronting these schools. Teachers and students join with administrators in determining policies about such matters as smoking, pupil evaluation, and use of space, as long as decisions are not illegal or in violation of school board policy. The principal has one vote in the assembly, but may veto its actions, subject to an override by a two-thirds vote of the whole. These assemblies, modeled after state and federal governments, with an executive, a legislative, and a judicial branch, are demonstrating that schools can not only teach about democracy, they can *be* democracies. In fact, these schools raise the question of whether it is possible for a school to teach democracy through nondemocratic means.

Alaskan small schools are places to watch, too. Their isolation makes them promising laboratories, uncontaminated by the rest of the world, for growing all sorts of unusual cultures. For instance, in Alaska, where one might routinely find a K–12 school staffed by three or four adults, no one knows that teachers are not supposed to be leaders. In many schools, all teachers, whether called *teacher, teaching-principal,* or *principal,* enjoy schoolwide leadership over issues from leaky roofs to parent involvement.

And many parochial schools thrive under what is often referred to as *servant leadership* on the part of the principal or headmaster. Principals, like parish priests, lead adults by serving adults. This invariably means involving teachers in important decisions of the schools. It is impossible to serve teachers by excluding them.

Quaker schools, too, have traditionally worked with great success by creating for students and adults a culture of participatory leadership, similar to the leadership of Quaker meetings. They assume that everyone has an "inner light," something to offer the group, if given the opportunity. And every member has something to learn from others. Members work together as equals, sharing ideas, planning, giving feedback, and supporting each other in new efforts. Leaders emerge in various ways at various times and then give way to other leaders. The work and the leadership of the group is a responsibility and an opportunity for all, as one observer at a faculty meeting in a Massachusetts Friends school discovered:

One teacher sat down in the large circle of staff with a box of tangled yarn which had been donated for art projects. The teacher quietly took a mass of the yarn and began winding it into a ball, while listening to and discussing staff issues. Soon the person on her left reached into the box and began unraveling and winding another ball of yarn. The person to her right did the same, and soon the yarn had spread around the circle with *everyone* winding while participating in the meeting. No one had ever said a word about the yarn.

These examples suggest that it is possible for adults and students in schools to work and lead together, to everyone's benefit. A community of leaders—neither a new nor an imaginary concept—seems foreign only to the majority of public schools in this country.

Conclusion

. . . I found out that those geese can fly from way up north to way down south, and back again. But they cannot do it alone, you see. It's something they must do in *community*. Oh, I know, it's a popular notion, and people swell with pride and emotion to think of themselves on the eagle side—strong, self-confident, solitary. Not bad traits. But we are what we are—that's something we can't choose. And though many of us would like to be seen as the eagle, I think God made us more like The Goose [Stomberg, 1982, p. 1].

The relationship between teacher and principal is currently under sharp scrutiny. The top-down model is too unwieldy, is subject to too much distortion, and is too unprofessional. Problems are frequently too big and too numerous for any one person to address alone. Schools need to recognize and develop many different kinds of leadership among many different kinds of people to replace the venerable, patriarchal model.

School leadership can come from principals who transform adversaries into colleagues; from teachers who individually or collectively take responsibility for the well-being of the school; from parents who translate a basic concern for their children into constructive actions; and from students who guide tours or in other ways offer community service. School leadership, then, can realistically be considered not only in terms of roles but also in terms of functions. Schoolpeople with different titles frequently share similar goals and tasks and need the same skills in enlisting disparate individuals and groups in a search for good schools.

Each school faces the task of constructing an effective educational and intellectual community around a unique set of issues and individuals. What is needed is leadership from within, from parents, teachers, principals, and students. Coalition building and the replacement of competitive relationships with collegial ones does not occur easily, let alone naturally. Schoolpeople need skills, insight, and vision that will equip them to assume responsibility for their schools. Such tools are seldom won through experience as classroom teachers or principals, or in courses at schools of education. Yet they are skills and values that educators committed to the importance—and inevitability—of many forms of leadership at the school level can develop.

Leaders need to be able to set general directions and create environments and structures that enable everyone in the school community to discover their own skills and talents and thereby be free to help students discover theirs. For students' needs will not be fully addressed until teachers and administrators together have worked out their own. This role must be one of enabling rather than controlling. Shared school leadership is a timely, volatile, and I think very promising issue for the improvement of schools from within, because public schools are strapped for adequate personal resources at the same time that extraordinary personal resources lie unacknowledged, untapped, unrewarded, and undeveloped within each schoolhouse.

I have suggested a reconfiguration of the relationships among student, teacher, and principal. A community of leaders offers independence, interdependence, resourcefulness, and collegiality. While much of the current literature suggests that effective principals are the heroes of the organization, I suspect that more often effective principals enable others to provide strong leadership. The best principals are not heroes; they are hero makers.

Few of the tea leaves before us suggest that public schools are heading toward communities of leaders. But the important question is not what our schools will become, but what they might be. There is a critical difference. The question of what will be implies the exercise of purely rational faculties, calling for trend analyses, projections, extrapolations, and probability curves. A view of what could be is not confined to these means. It embraces intuition, creativity, morality, reason, and above all, vision. It extends inquiry from the realm of the probable to the realm of the possible. Clear vision offers inventive, promising, and powerful ideas for improving schools from within.

ELEVEN

Visions of Good Schools

While rummaging through a local newspaper in rural Maine, I came upon an advertisement in the "used farm equipment" section: "For sale, Model 95 International Harvester Hay Baler, $900 as is. Working, but could work better."

"Working, but could work better" is a phrase that might also be applied to our public schools. This condition has generated an extraordinary number and variety of conceptions of quality in schools during the past decade. "Effective schools," "excellent schools," "essential schools," and "successful schools" are a few of the current code words.

I have suggested how gifted and talented schoolpeople can be at resisting, subverting, and ignoring foreign prescriptions for the improvement of their schools. If the many conceptions of good schools in the current literature are destined to be fended off by school practitioners—or, at best, to be distorted by them to serve local purposes in a manner that would probably distress Ronald Edmonds, Mortimer Adler, and William Bennett—then what conception of schools and schooling will prevail? Where will we derive an organizing principle, a sense of moral order? Is there a vision of good education that those who work in the schools *will* take seriously?

I think there is. I would like to consider here the conception of a desirable school, the vision of a good school that every teacher and principal harbors. The personal vision of school practitioners is a kind of moral imagination that gives them the ability to see schools not as they are, but as they would like them to become. I find practitioners' personal

147

visions usually deeply submerged, sometimes fragmentary, and seldom articulated. A painful pause usually awaits anyone who asks a teacher or principal, "What is your vision for a good school?" But I am convinced the vision is there. I find that it usually emerges when schoolpeople complete sentences like: "When I leave this school I would like to be remembered for . . ."; "I want my school to become a place where . . ."; "The kind of school I would like my own children to attend would . . ."; or "The kind of school I would like to teach in . . . ." A personal vision, then, is one's overall conception of what the educator wants the organization to stand for; what its primary mission is; what its basic, core values are; a sense of how all the parts fit together; and, above all, how the vision maker fits into the grand plan.

Dreams can come to us in the day as well as the night. The night dreams are often a journey back into the repressed unconscious. Daydreams, on the other hand, are the occasion of a journey forward, toward what might be, what can be, what we want to be. Call them personal visions. I can think of nothing so conspicuously missing in the effort to improve our schools as the continuous engagement of teachers and principals in constructing visions—in contemplating, for instance, what constitutes desirable leadership, what children should learn, and what the teaching profession might become.

All of us begin our work in education with a 20/20 personal vision about the way we would like a school to be. This is what we value and are prepared to work and even fight for. That is why we became educators. Then, by about December of our first year, something devastating and apparently inevitable begins to happen. Our personal vision becomes blurred by the well-meaning expectations and lists of others. Superintendents, state departments of education, and universities often all but obliterate the personal visions of teachers and principals with their own abundant goals and objectives. The capacity to retain and adhere to a personal vision becomes blunted by exhaustion and compliance. It becomes painful to have what we care deeply about repeat-

edly violated or discounted. So, our visions take refuge way
down in our hip pockets where, in too many cases, they forever languish rather than inspire.

A few years ago, I spent a day on Cape Cod with a
number of schoolpeople to try to retrieve our visions. One of
the participants, a veteran teacher of many years and wars,
put it well: "It's gotten so that what's *me* is hard to figure out
anymore." The difference between an educator and a middle
manager, between a leader and a bureaucrat, between a
teacher and a teaching machine, seems to be that the one
operates from a personal vision as a guiding "independent
variable," while the other responds to the demands of others
as a subservient "dependent variable."

As principal, I too found myself, after a while, suc-
cumbing to what I came to call my *PTA rhetoric*. In addresses
to parent groups, I found myself using words like *discipline,
rigor, work, basics, standards*. All hard, harsh, legitimate-sound-
ing words that revealed less of my personal vision and more
of what I thought parents and others wanted to hear. In short,
I found myself, as most other teachers and principals do,
becoming more obsessively practical while becoming less
visionary. PTA rhetoric is all too abundant in our schools.

It is not easy to identify, let alone reveal, what we believe in, but that day on Cape Cod, I was able to begin to rediscover and to clarify my vision. I found that a good school
for me is not a prescription for others, but a dream for myself
and my children. Prescriptions for other people's children,
important as they may be, have a different level of meaning
and commitment. Prescriptions for ourselves and for our kin
come out of deeply personal as well as professional roots.
"The kind of school I would like my children to attend . . ."
carries with it a most profound kind of accountability.

The Importance of School Practitioners' Visions

So, why struggle to restore, to uncover, and to honor
the personal visions of schoolpeople? In recent years, I have
exchanged and celebrated visions with school teachers and

principals on many occasions. In considering and analyzing the many elements of our different visions, I find common qualities and much that could prove of benefit to educational reform. I have suggested that massive research studies stand little chance of having a major and direct influence on the loosely coupled world of schools. One reason to honor the visions of schoolpeople, then, is that these are the prescriptions for school reform that have the best chance to be taken seriously, enacted, and sustained by teachers and principals.

There is a second reason. Research frequently provides a broad view, badly needed in schools. Yet, the data base is, in many respects, thin. Researchers pay brief visits to many schools, asking few questions of a large sample, frequently with all the effect of a tea bag swished through a bathtub. The visions of schoolpeople, by contrast, stem from many years' experience in perhaps only one or two school settings. I agree with the researcher who said, "Believable answers to important questions can be generated with $N = 1$." I find that virtually everyone who works in a school 190 days a year for several years develops extraordinary practical knowledge about such matters as the curriculum, child development, discipline, leadership, desegregation, and parent involvement. And these rich insights, hammered out of years of practice, give richness and credibility to the visions schoolpeople hold about good education. Strong tea indeed.

A third reason I believe it is essential to elicit the visions that school practitioners carry with them about reforming their schools is that, as I vividly recall, the excitement of working in schools, the satisfactions, the rewards come from studying a difficult situation and then generating one's own plan for improving things. Why should educators be placed— or place themselves—in the position of only implementing the grand ideas of others, ideas with which they may not agree? Nothing is more toxic to the development of a community of learners or a community of leaders. The greatest tragedy I know is to be caught every day in the position of doing something one does not want to do or does not believe in. As we saw at the outset, too many educators are playing out this tragedy, functioning as assembly-line robots whose main business is production, not learning. This condition, above everything else, diminishes both learning and professionalism in the public schools.

Teachers and principals who convey their craft knowledge and their visions to other adults derive enormous personal satisfaction and recognition. Vision unlocked is energy unlocked. Despite the good rhetoric about the importance of school teachers and principals offered in recent state and national reform proposals, few schoolpeople feel valued or recognized for their work. That is not what the local press, the PTA, or the central office convey each day. Yet, of all the pressing needs of public school practitioners, none is more vital than the need for personal and professional recognition from a society that values an education far more than it values those who provide it. For work in schools to become a profession, teachers and principals must feel professionally recognized. Recognition can come from inviting schoolpeople to share their craft knowledge with colleagues and others, from writing about practice, from allowing them to make major decisions, from enabling them to become mentors to others who would like to become capable of teaching and leading— and, above all, from creating and revealing and working toward their personal vision.

Another reason to take the concept of vision seriously is that the personal visions of adults, no matter how fragmented and rudimentary, are not inconsequential to the education of youngsters. Many researchers are finding a consistent relationship between the presence of teachers' and principals' visions and the effectiveness of their schools. Joan Lipsitz, for instance, concluded that "Extracting effective school practices from one setting and replicating them elsewhere may make a bad school mediocre. To become a good school requires a change in vision from within" (1984, p. 216). After extensive observation of eight very good—and very different—elementary school principals, Blumberg and Greenfield (1980) concluded that one characteristic shared by all of them was that they had a vision for their schools that was noble, realistic, and clear. If the self-evident is not convincing, the literature, then, offers ample testimony to the central place of internal visions in school improvement.

Another good reason for schoolpeople to formulate and articulate their own visions of the way their schools ought to be is that by *not* doing so, they invite random prescription from outside: from the central office, from the state department of education, from national commissions and task forces. There is already too much random behavior in schools. I believe that very few of these outsiders really want to run the schools. They certainly are not going to stay around to monitor things. Most only want to be sure that teachers and principals have a sense of where they are going and are running the schools thoughtfully and deliberately so they will get there. A school without visions is a vacuum inviting intrusion. A school that proclaims its own vision achieves and deserves some measure of what they call *diplomatic immunity* in Washington.

I know of no teacher, principal, counselor, social worker, department head, or librarian who does not have at least a rudimentary sense of the kind of classroom or school he or she would like to see. Many have well-developed visions of the kinds of places in which they would like to have their own children study or in which they themselves would like to work. It often appears that the visions of good education proffered by the national commissions and task forces land in a desert, but this is misleading. In fact, most new ideas from without must compete with fiercely held, albeit covert, conceptions already in place.

However, those who work in the schools cannot have it both ways, dismissing the many conceptions of good schools that currently bombard them but still refusing to reveal their own visions or goals and approaches for achieving them. If teachers and principals do not want to be the dependent variable in attempts to improve the schools, they will have to become the independent variable. In schools, treading water is no longer an option. Schoolpeople must either propel themselves in some direction, be towed, or sink.

Where Are the Visions of Schoolpeople?

Given the many compelling reasons for inclusion of the thinking of schoolpeople, it is astonishing to me that the voices and visions of teachers and principals are not more audible and visible in the current discussions and debates about school improvement. It is unthinkable that any other profession undergoing the same close scrutiny would allow all the descriptions of practice, analyses of practice, and prescriptions for improving practice to come only from outsiders looking in. Where are the voices of the insiders? Why can't we walk into a school and see and hear the mission of that school conveyed with clarity and conviction in corridors and classrooms? How can the professionals who work in schools rally around a common purpose? Under what conditions will their individual and collective visions be formulated and revealed? What will enable teachers and administrators to take their own visions seriously, have confidence in them, and act on them?

One response to these questions lies in a conversation I recently had with a group of principals. During the course of this discussion, someone asked why principals fail, by and large, to convey in their schools, through their actions and language, a clear vision and sense of purpose. The answers were revealing.

"Perhaps because principals have no mission and sense of purpose—no theoretical, guiding principle," said one.

"I'm afraid that expressing my conception of a good school would stir up trouble within the school," said another. "Any idea I put forth would inevitably be at odds with the ideas of some teachers or parents or the central office. And then what?"

"I guess I don't telegraph my vision because of a feeling of powerlessness, lack of credibility—perhaps I fear that no one would take it seriously, especially outside the building," said a third. "It's pretentious. After all, I don't have the authority or national stature of a Boyer or a Goodlad."

"It's because so many of us see ourselves as middle

managers whose responsibility it is to transmit the ideas, goals, and visions of those above us," one principal explained. "It's inappropriate to introduce my own ideas about school reform into the formula. They're not wanted and not needed."

"I have a pretty clear vision of how I would like my school to be in, say, five years," commented another, "but, strategically, it is unwise to pull all my cards out at once. Better to unveil portions of my vision incrementally. The total idea would startle, threaten, or offend others. After five years, it will all be visible."

Finally, one principal noted, "I *am* working on a vision—but to be worth a damn it has to be a vision that comes from and reflects the thinking of the whole school community. It's a very complicated process to try to find a consensus where at the moment little exists. If and when we find that consensus, I'll be the first to engrave it over the door of the school."

These comments identify some of the complexities and the formidable obstacles to the development of a school-based vision and a school-based plan for improvement. I believe that, under the right conditions, schoolpeople will think through for themselves what they want their schools to become and their place in the process, and then set out with conviction to make their visions a reality. And I think that trying to find these conditions holds more promise for improving elementary and secondary schools from within than trying to work through the resistance that accompanies attempts to impose an orthodoxy from without.

How to encourage teachers and principals to continuously consider, reflect on, and articulate their visions about what their classrooms and schools might become is a formidable job, one that is right at the heart of school improvement. When I consider the concept of personal vision with teachers and principals, a number of questions recur:

Why worry about vision? What are the advantages for teachers and principals of being in touch with their visions? What do students gain when the adults with whom they work are visionaries? What are the disadvantages of holding and sharing a vision? What is the relationship between a personal vision and a collective vision? Where do visions come from and how can they be developed? How can one person be a part of another person's vision? How is vision translated into practice? Exploration of these questions offers rich possibilities for researchers, consultants, academics, and school leaders who would contribute to this unusual route toward school reform.

And then there are more personal, practical, and compelling questions that confront any person intent on becoming a vision maker.

Do I have *a personal vision?* This was a frightening question for me and for others on the Cape. I am now convinced that everyone who works within a school has, beneath the PTA rhetoric, at least the rudiments of a personal vision. It may be fragmentary; it may not be elegant; it may never be asked for; but it is there.

What are the essential elements of my personal vision? We in education are so overwhelmed with good and bad ideas that it is difficult to find the artichoke heart inside the foliage. By what means can educators distill the essence of their often-diffuse visions? Anyone who has worked in a school knows it is impossible to move on a dozen fronts at once. School improvement emanating from a small number of clear priorities is more possible and powerful.

Once revealed, how can I sharpen and develop my vision and make it coherent, respectable, and legitimate for others and especially for myself? Perhaps the biggest contribution of the recent national reports may be to provide a background against which all of us can develop our own visions. We should use these conceptions and not be used by them. The crisis under which schools suffer is, above all, a crisis of self-confidence. How then can schoolpeople elevate their visions to the pedestal they deserve, alongside the visions of Goodlad, Boyer, Sizer, and Adler?

What would happen if I flew my vision from the flagpole in front of the school? What happens when I reveal and act on my vision? As we have seen, schoolpeople live under a taboo against revealing their craft knowledge and their visions to others. Or, as a fortune cookie once advised me, "For every vision there will be an equal and opposite *re*vision!" Educators fear exposing their visions because they believe their visions will violate the visions of others. This will cause arguments and conflict for everyone. Schools already have too much anguish. Under what conditions, then, will teachers and principals take the risk of violating this taboo?

And under what conditions might the visions of others within the school—administrators, teachers, parents, students— be elicited? Is it possible for a school to become a community of visionaries? Individuals always treasure their own visions, but other people's visions need to be carefully watched! Superintendents, principals, and teachers, by and large, have not been successful in eliciting leadership from those who occupy the rung below them on the authority ladder. How might they find more success in eliciting visions? In talking with educators, I find that personal visions are seldom asked for and do not appear to be valued by superiors. Principals report, for instance, that "my superintendent has never invited me to share *my* vision for a good school." Yet, paradoxically, when I speak to superintendents they convey a totally different message: "I'd give anything to have these principals figure out what they stand for, and then stand there with conviction and with courage." Many teachers and principals would say the same thing about the other. Our visions seem to be what those we work for value least, yet what those who work for and with us seem to desperately seek and value the most. But it is not always that simple. How, I wonder, to resolve this paradox?

And how might I reconcile my vision with the expectations and visions of the many others in my school? Honoring the visions of others, maintaining fidelity to one's own vision, and at the same time working toward a collective vision and coherent institutional purpose constitute an extraordinary definition of school leadership and represent one of the most important undertakings facing those who would improve schools from within.

One reason visions have gone underground is that when they emerge aboveground they are trampled. Under what conditions can these many, varied, fragile, vital sprouts grow and flourish together in the same garden? We need to recognize that there are abundant vision killers at large out there and within our schools. Otherwise personal visions would be as prevalent as crabgrass. One is the wet blanket: "Are you crazy?" "They'll never let us!" "We've tried that and it didn't work!" "Who are *you* to say that?" There are many cynics in the schools whose dreams have been dashed and who now take a peculiar delight in dashing the dreams of others.

Another vision killer is the tendency of schools to jump to premature implementation. "If it's a good idea, let's do it tomorrow." I find it takes a while for visions to steep, to be savored, to permeate, to be enjoyed and celebrated before we subject them to the hard knocks that come with improving schools. Visions need to take root before we attempt to strip them of their fruit.

Another vision killer is the tendency to be too hopeful, entertaining high or exacting expectations for visions that, of course, are doomed to disappointment and failure. Developing one's personal vision of schools is a never-ending process. Therefore, sharing a vision means sharing an incomplete conception that might change before the ink is dry on the page. To expose one's own vision, knowing it is never static and never complete, constitutes, then, a double risk. It is risky to share something as vulnerable, intimate, and important as one's vision; it is even more risky to put something out there that will never be a finished product, but that will always be an approximation. Where will the courage to take this greatest of risks come from?

Preserving One's Vision

How, then, can educators come to live with the hope of their visions in the midst of the hopelessness of ever completely fulfilling them? A vision for me is like a star or a compass. It offers a clear, sometimes shining sense of direction, a destination. It is important, therefore, not to ask, "Have we reached the star yet or are we at 'north' yet?" The more realistic and helpful question is, "How much closer to the star or to the compass course are we today than we were last week?" One way or another, it is important to heed the advice of one visionary teacher: "We must find ways to kill the vision killers so rampant in our schools." This is a crucial and often overlooked element of improving schools.

These are some of the troublesome issues that seem to accompany vision making among schoolpeople. A definition of school I like very much is "four walls surrounding a future." This image captures nicely the essence of what school improvement means for me in my work. I believe that the character and quality of schools will dramatically improve when, and if, those who work in schools—teachers, students, parents, and administrators—come in touch with one another, with their personal visions, and with the way they would like their schools to be, and then take deliberate steps to move toward them. This is school improvement emerging from *within* the four walls of the schoolhouse. Visions will come from within us—or not at all. We will wait forever in futility for someone to provide us with a vision, as one schoolperson conveyed so eloquently in a lovely piece of writing:

A Thousand Miles

I traveled a thousand miles to find a vision. I came to the citadel of learning, for surely Harvard would have the vision I needed. I asked and probed and thought and reflected. I questioned and looked from person to person.

I found visions. Many of them. They came in all sorts of shapes and sizes. They were large ones and modest ones. There were complex ones and simple ones. They all seem to fit—yet none of them fit me. Why?

Then I remembered that I once had a vision—a vision that was my very own. Where had it gone? What had I done with it? So I started searching those long dark corridors of past years.

I found my vision. Rusty, dirty from lack of care—but still there. It was my vision, a vision not exactly like anyone else's. With the power to carry me forward, to shine light on the path of the future—for me and for those with whom I might share my vision.

And I learned an important lesson. I learned that each of us must have a vision. It must be uniquely ours. For until we have a vision to share, we can't understand anyone else's. I learned I must keep my vision polished brightly through daily attention, or I will lose it again. That it can act as a guiding beacon only as long as I hold it in front of me.

And I discovered that I can look to myself. That I am rich in resources and thoughts and ideas. That the future, my future, lies not out there but inside me.

Nothing so professionalizes work in schools as educators who create within the schoolhouse visions of good education. Everyone who works in a school is not only entitled to a unique and personal vision of the way he or she would like the school to become, but has an obligation to uncover, discover, and rediscover what that vision is and contribute it to the betterment of the school community. A middle school teacher said it all: "I need to be part of the forest-creating. I like seeing the whole picture and helping guide toward it."

Ultimately, there are probably two workable strategies for improving the schools: somehow to get teachers and principals to work on closing the gap between the way their schools are and the way people outside these schools would have them be; or to work toward closing the gap between the way the schools are and the way those within the schools would like them to be. Both paths raise questions and problems. I think that the greater promise for school reform—and sufficient resources to achieve it—now resides within the schools. Changes in schools may be initiated from without, but the most important and most lasting changes will come from within.

Schools *are* capable of improving themselves. If the conditions are right, I am confident that teachers and principals and parents can work together to influence schools in ways others cannot. One of these conditions is the creation of visions. The Old Testament tells us that "a people without a vision shall perish." The same can be said about schools and schoolpeople without visions. It might also be said that schools full of vision will flourish.

TWELVE

A Personal Vision

In the past two decades, educators have seen the focus shift from the question, Do schools make any difference?, to the far more hopeful question, What characteristics of schools are associated with what desirable outcome for students, teachers, and principals? Everyone seems to have a distinctive response.

For several years, I too have been struggling to clarify and articulate my own vision of a good school. I have exchanged, analyzed, and celebrated personal visions with schoolpeople on many occasions. Little by little, from these conversations, from my own work in schools, from visits to other schools, from reading, writing, and teaching, the important pieces of my personal vision have emerged. Much of it has been infused in the preceding pages. I would like to conclude by trying to make explicit here what matters most to me about schools.

Not surprisingly, my conception of a good school is one where I would like to teach or be a principal; it is the school that I would be proud to be remembered for helping to create. It is also the school that I, as a parent, would like my daughters to attend. Mine is a personal vision, a conception of what might be, what could be, perhaps what should be, rather than a projection of what will be. I find this continuous exercise of vision making to be engaging, fun, often useful, and above all, hopeful. Those of us who work in or near public schools need hope.

A Community of Learners

Most of the other pieces of my vision relate to this central idea. A school as a community of learners is the "coat rack" on which are hung many supporting components and to which all the other pieces are fastened. There is much talk these days about the importance of student achievement, of teachers' staff development, and of principals' professional growth as if all of these learners inhabit different planets. A good school for me is a place where everyone is teaching and everyone is learning—simultaneously, under the same roof. Students are teaching and learning; principals are teaching and learning; and teachers are teaching and learning. Everything that goes on in school contributes to this end. School need not merely be a place where there are big people who are learn*ed* and little people who are learn*ers*.

In a community of learners, the principal occupies a central place, not as the "headmaster" or "head teacher" suffering under the "burden of ascribed omniscience." Rather, the principal is the head learner engaging in, displaying, and modeling the behavior we expect and hope teachers and students will adopt. This is the kind of school system like one on the West Coast where the superintendent instructed all the principals: "I expect you to spend one day a week somewhere, somehow, devoted to your own learning, your professional development."

That teachers and principals and students are learning, then, is far more important to the development of a community of learners than *what* they are learning. A major responsibility of adults in a community of learners is to actively engage in their own learning, to make their learning visible to youngsters and to other adults alike, to enjoy and celebrate this learning, and to sustain it over time even—especially—when swamped by the demands of others and by their work.

Individuals enter into collaborative relationships only after they come to realize that they cannot achieve what they want to achieve acting alone. I think many teachers and principals have reached that point. Principals alone cannot "inservice" teachers any more than teachers can ensure that all their students will be voracious learners. Principals, teachers, students, and parents working together, on the other hand, can create within their schools an ecology of reflection, growth, and refinement of practice—a community of learners.

Collegiality

My years in school suggest that the quality of adult relationships within a school has more to do with the quality and character of the school and with the accomplishments of students than any other factor. In too many schools, personal relationships tend to be adversarial relationships: teacher against student, teacher against teacher, principal against teacher, and schoolpeople against parents. The most memorable schools I visit are ones that have begun to find ways of transforming these adversarial and "parallel play" relationships into cooperative and collegial coalitions.

I was impressed last summer while out bluefishing with a professional charter captain (also a high school teacher) by his response when we found ourselves in the middle of a school of blues. He immediately got on the marine radio and reported our good fortune and position to the hundreds of other fishermen on Nantucket Sound. I commented on the difference between this generosity and what we often find among teachers and principals in their schools. "Oh," he said, "that's what I do for bluefish. But the striped bass— that's another story." Even those who pride themselves on their collegiality have their stripers!

The kind of school I would like to work in and have my children attend, the kind of school I suspect most teachers and principals would like to be part of, is, in contrast, a place where teachers and principals talk with one another about practice, observe one another engaged in their work, share their craft knowledge with each other, and actively help each other become better. In a collegial school, adults and students are constantly learning because everyone is a staff developer for everyone else.

Risk Taking

My vision of a good school is one where students and adults are encouraged to take risks, and where a safety net protects those who risk. The "nation" may be at risk, and many students are described as "at risk," but this certainly does not describe the cautious culture of our schools. The lives of teachers and principals are more closely akin to one definition of a mushroom: "You're kept in the dark most of the time, periodically you're covered with manure, and when you stick your head out it gets chopped off." Yet if we want students to be less docile and more inventive and adventuresome in their thinking, then adults must model risk taking as well as learning. If we want to improve schools, we must risk doing things differently next September than we did them last September. New, unusual ideas must be viewed not as a nuisance or embarrassment, but as a sign of life.

Considerable research suggests that risk taking is highly associated with learning. Indeed, when I consider my own most profound learning experiences, I find that they were occasions when I was out on a limb, where the boat was heeling and water coming over the gunwales. Learning seldom comes from passively, safely sitting still in the water with the sails flapping.

I see evidence that many adults and children in schools would like to take more risks, while at the same time their schools seem to launder out risk taking. The most powerful learning experiences for members of the Principals' Center, for instance, continue to be the most risky. Visits to one another's schools, writing about practice, and leading workshops all stand in contrast to the more prevalent, antiseptic, risk-free pedagogy wonderfully labeled by one Texas staff developer, "sit and git."

I am reminded of the doctoral candidate who came into the elementary school where I was teaching many years ago. She was writing her dissertation on the little conversation (little dance, really) that takes place when a teacher comes to a principal and asks permission to try some new idea—say, taking a field trip by boat around the Farralon Islands seaward of the Golden Gate. Her research revealed a remarkably consistent protocol of responses.

The initial response of the principal was a body language of furled brow, worried look, bent shoulders. If this posture was not enough to stifle the idea, the next response was a parade of the litany of reasons why not—all the problems the implementation of such an idea would cause. "What about the other fourth grade across the hall?" "How does this fit into the scope and sequence of the required curriculum?" "The last time we took a field trip by boat two children got seasick and I'm still hearing from the school board." We all know the list.

The principal's next response, if the poor teacher is still enthusiastic, is, "Well, let me think about it. Get back to me in a couple of weeks." Stall. If the teacher should somehow return undeterred in a couple of weeks, the response is apt to be, "Okay, you may take the field trip, *but* if anything happens, I want you to know it's *your* responsibility."

It is not only the imaginative and creative teacher who encounters these roadblocks, of course. It is what the principal who wants to develop a new pupil evaluation system hears from the superintendent; it is what the student who wants to interview merchants in the neighborhood rather than read books for a social studies report hears from the teacher. This pathologically cautious behavior is endemic to our schools. What kind of climate for risk taking and for learning are we promoting with these responses to new ideas? Good for mushrooms, perhaps, but not for a community of learners.

The Chinese use the same ideograph to represent the concept of "danger" as they use for the idea "opportunity," recognizing that since opportunity and danger always occur together, their symbols should also be inseparable. This ancient culture, unlike the culture of schools, recognizes that it is impossible to make a significant move forward without encountering risks. The scent of danger and risk should alert us, therefore, to the fact that we may be headed in the right rather than the wrong direction.

The only good question, it seems to me, to ask of the teacher who would take that risky field trip is, "What do you think the children might learn from it?" That is the high ground. A casual response of "Well, the kids have worked hard all year . . ." is cause for caution. A considered response that integrates the geography unit with the biology unit with writing is convincing. And a convincing response is the cue for the principal to not only approve the trip but to provide a safety net by conveying that "we" will share responsibility for it. I would like to work in, or have my daughters attend, such a school.

Why then do we persist in laundering risk taking from our schools? If we are serious about learning for ourselves and others, then we must become serious about risk taking—for ourselves and others. When the risks are high, when hooked into a safety line, the learning curve goes off the chart, as any Outward Bound participant can attest.

Recommitment

A good school, for me, is one where each adult has chosen to be. Pupils live under a compulsory attendance law. They must come to school. Most adults *feel* every bit as conscripted. Yet, we all know that people who are going through the motions (such as the teacher I recently overheard who lamented, "Only eighteen more years 'til I retire") do not make very good teachers or administrators.

The crisis in education for schoolpeople is less one of commitment than of *recommitment*. The highly routinized nature of school work, in time, tends to make automatons of us all. A vital question is, Who can do what to provide opportunities for periodic recommitment for those who work in schools so that work will remain a vital profession and not become a tedious job?

A request by any teacher for a leave of absence for any purpose, for instance, should be granted. The teacher is requesting an opportunity to stop, reflect, replenish, and consider other options. If the teacher chooses to return to the school, everyone wins—the teacher, students, school. If the teacher decides to leave, everyone wins. Sabbaticals would be preferable, but automatic availability of leaves of absence without pay can also help relieve the trapped feeling so prevalent among schoolpeople. A school full of indentured servants is not the school I would like to work in or be remembered for.

A good friend of mine was, for many years, principal of a demanding inner city school in New Orleans. I remember visiting her one day, when, out of the blue, she said, "Let's go for a walk." As we walked along the Mississippi River, she relayed to me that once each week she leaves her building, fully paid, during school time, and declares "my one-hour sabbatical." During this "sabbatical," she contemplates her career, her school, and then decides (or not) to return. Usually, she creates for herself the aura of choice. And, choosing to return, she embarks again, recommitted to her important work.

Many principals in Newfoundland—a bright, willful, ornery, independent lot—have worked out a creative solution to the problem of conscription. They may choose to work for reduced pay—say three-fourths salary for three years—and then take a leave of absence the fourth year at three-fourths salary, to build a boat, go fishing, or travel. Others take four-fifths pay for four years, with the fifth year off at four-fifths pay. It costs the system no more, and everyone wins. Schoolpeople badly need a repertoire of other ways that would enable them to recommit, to make deliberate choices to be there. The only difference between a rut and a grave is the depth of the hole.

As a principal, each year I met with each staff member and asked, "If you could decide under ideal conditions what you would like to do next year and with whom, what would it be?" I provided one boundary condition: Teachers had to work in the school in some way with children. In short, I invited teachers to disregard all practical constraints for a few moments and reflect on their work as educators, consider current interests, ideas, skills, and relationships, and engage in some "if only . . ." brainstorming. My objective was for all of us to come to school each September with at least one significant new element in our professional and personal lives— something about which to dream, think, worry, get excited, risk, and remain alive.

Many teachers expressed the wish to do "the same

thing next year." But more teachers came ready to dream. A teacher aide wants to become a librarian; a teacher wants to become a principal; three teachers want to work together. It came as a surprise to us how closely we were able to comply with most of these "daydreams." The results suggest that following the best interest of teachers is often in the best interest of their students and the school. Teachers do not have to spend another year doing the same thing in the same place in the same way. Change nourishes recommitment. Fundamental, periodic choice replenishes the profession and the professional.

Respect for Diversity

My vision for a school is one that offers great respect for differences among people. Different people—teachers, parents, students, and principals—like it and learn better that way. Often, differences in schools are unacknowledged, by placing the burden on students or teachers to comply with the uniform expectations of the school. And often differences *are* accepted, as a painful fact of life in which each teacher, for instance, must live with the bottom ability group, or with the kids from the other side of the tracks, and in which each principal must live with that "lemon" teacher. More often, we furtively try to "group out" differences as fast as they emerge.

I would prefer my children to be in a school where differences were looked for, attended to, and celebrated as good news, as opportunities for learning. The question with which so many are preoccupied in schools is, What are the limits of diversity beyond which behavior is unacceptable? It is an important question, but the question I would like to see asked more often is, How can we make conscious, deliberate use of differences in social class, gender, age, ability, race, and interests as resources for learning? Differences, like risk taking, hold great opportunities for learning. Differences offer a free, abundant, and renewable resource, as we observe at the Principals' Center when leaders from urban, rural, suburban, public, private, parochial, elementary, middle, and high schools all sit around the same table.

I would like to see our disdain for differences among students replaced by the question, How can we make use of the differences for the powerful learning opportunity they hold? In the same way, I would like to see our compulsion for eliminating differences among teachers and among schools replaced with the question, How can we deliberately make use of these differences to improve schools? The teacher interested in restoring fire safety *is* different in many ways from the teacher who would turn the library into a media center. Differences of philosophy, style, and passion are remarkable sources for school improvement. What is important about people—and about schools—is what is different, not what is the same.

A Place for Philosophers

The kind of school that I envision is one that offers a special place for philosophers, for people who ask "why" questions. Nothing is more important to building a culture of inquiry and a community of learners. Why are there twenty-five children in every class? Why are the upper grades upstairs and the lower grades downstairs? Why do adults talk 80 percent of the time and students 30 percent of the time when students outnumber adults by a ratio of 25 to 1? In schools, there *are* philosophers, usually the five- and six-year-olds. But very soon they turn from philosophers into producers. Too bad. For everyone.

How can we come to see common practices in schools not as encrusted regularities, as "wallpaper patterns," but rather as tentative decisions subject to continuous examinations and review? I think it is possible to set up mechanisms in schools that allow us to continuously examine and question our embedded, routinized ways of doing things. For instance, teachers and parents new to a school—usually subtly told to be seen but not heard for a couple of years—instead might convey what they so clearly see and hear around them.

Then all of us might find better reasons for doing what we did last September again next September. Above all, philosophers residing under the roof of the schoolhouse can constantly juxtapose the way things are with fresh visions of what they might become.

Humor

Schools are funny places. A lot of funny things happen there. I would like to be part of a school in which a great deal is made of humor. Humor is sorely lacking in this profession, in textbooks and educational writing, in research, in state departments, in universities—and in schools. Yet, humor, like risk taking and diversity, is highly related to learning and the development of intelligence, not to mention quality of life. And humor can be a glue that binds an assorted group of individuals into a community. People learn and grow and survive through humor. We should make an effort to elicit and cultivate it, rather than ignore, thwart, or merely tolerate it.

One principal I know keeps a little journal of funny, ridiculous things he hears about the school. I borrowed it recently and found some memorable entries. PE teacher to children on the playground: "Okay, kids, line up in a circle." Another teacher: "Okay, kids, pair up by threes." When I was a principal, during one cold month of March—heated only by teachers who were not reappointed—I was working in my office late one afternoon when a group of young boys arrived under my window on their bikes. As they were leaving, the smallest one yelled out, "Hey, wait for me, I'm your *leader*." Precisely how I was feeling as leader of the school! That anecdote, pasted on my bulletin board, helped get me through the rest of the year.

One middle school student purportedly wrote this description of the human body for a science class: "The body is composed of three parts: the brainium, the borax, and the abominable cavity. The brainium contains the brain; the borax contains the lungs, the liver, and the *other* living things; the abominable cavity contains the bowels, of which there are five: *A, E, I, O,* and *U.*" Unlike those in other professions—law, architecture, engineering—our clients parade an unending abundance of humor before us.

The medical profession too has something to say about humor: Laughter causes lungs to pump out carbon dioxide, eyes to cleanse themselves with tears, muscles to relax tension, adrenaline to increase, and the cardiovascular system to be exercised. Perhaps most important for those in schools, endorphins, which are chemicals produced by the brain to relieve pain, are released into the bloodstream when a person laughs. Clearly, laughter is good for schools and for those who inhabit them.

A Community of Leaders

One definition of leadership I like is "making happen that in which you believe." Principals believe in many things and make many of them happen. Few question that principals are leaders. But others in schools—teachers, librarians, guidance counselors, parents, and students—also want to make what *they* believe in happen. The kind of school I would like my children to attend is one where *everyone* gets a chance to be a leader. Various studies suggest that about 80 percent of first-grade students feel good about who they are. By sixth grade only 20 percent feel good about themselves. And, by the end of high school, perhaps 5 percent. Clearly, schools are not very good at helping students to feel self-confident, instrumental, and worthy. But a school can be far more than a place that allows only some students to serve on the student council or a place that encourages only a few teachers to be departmental chairs. School can be a place whose very mission is to ensure that everyone becomes a school leader in some ways and at some times in concert with some others. A school can fulfill no higher purpose than to teach all of its members that they can make what they believe in happen and to encourage them to contribute to and benefit from the leadership of others. A community of leaders is a vision of what might become a vital part of the school culture. But a community of leaders is far more than a piece of the professional school culture. Without shared leadership, it is impossible for a professional culture to exist in a school. And, as I have suggested earlier, with a community of leaders comes a community of learners.

Low Anxiety and High Standards

A final characteristic of a school in which I suspect many teachers, parents, and principals would like to work or that they would like their children to attend has to do with the relationship between anxiety and standards. Some schools are characterized by high anxiety and high standards—exam schools or many elite preparatory schools, for instance; some schools by low anxiety and low standards—some "free" schools, for example. Too many schools are characterized by high anxiety and low standards, an "everyone loses" combination. The condition of *low anxiety and high standards* is hardest to attain, least often seen, yet offers, I believe, the greatest possibilities for learning. Considerable research suggests that attention, learning, performance, retention, and recall all diminish when anxiety of the learner is high. Yet we in schools seem particularly adept at deliberately heightening anxiety through grades, homework, notes home, threat of failure, and exams, so that we may control student behavior.

While the spate of recent national and state efforts to reform the schools may indeed have raised standards a bit, I suspect they have raised anxiety much more. Extraordinary anxiety from parents, school boards, superintendents, the media, and state departments of education bombards schools from without. This makes it all the more important for those within to insulate from rather than conduct anxiety, to be anxiety reducers rather than anxiety generators.

Yet in the Boston area forty-nine students have been hospitalized in the past three years for school stress. Their symptoms vary from depression to suicidal tendencies, headaches, chest pains, and, of course, alcohol and drug abuse.

One high school student, after negotiating months of fifty-five-minute periods, bells, homework, reports, unmet obligations, late and detention slips, noted that, "I feel like a phonograph record designed for 33 1/3 RPM, constantly being played at 78 RPM." A teacher or principal might say the same.

What can we do to reduce anxiety and raise standards within schools? As a parent in an educational community that generates tremendous tension, one thing I did was write a letter to my daughter's principal:

Dear Marilyn,

I have been the recipient over the years of many assorted letters to the principal from Newton parents, so I thought I would try my hand at putting one together—about something that's been on my mind during the years our daughter Joanna has been a student at the High School.

Thus far, it has been a very stimulating and rich experience for her to associate daily with very able and earnest teachers and students. By most measures—yours and ours—she has been doing fine: grades, attendance, involvement, effort, and considerable learning.

A few days ago I read in the *Globe* of a major attempt by the Massachusetts Institute of Technology to redirect the focus of its programs. A paragraph in the story jumped out at me because it seemed to capture both a problem and a solution at MIT that has also been in the minds of all of us in Joanna's family: "President Gray said he is committed to a slight reduction in the throttle setting of undergraduate academic life. Because MIT tends to draw overachievers, he said such a reduction would provide a little more time on the margins . . . for reflection, pleasure, and interaction with colleagues."

I think Newton, no less than MIT, draws many overachieving students as well as what one administrator called "severely gifted" parents, who together tend constantly to *up* the throttle setting of high school academic life. More and more is demanded faster to be better and better, not only by parents to ensure college admission, but also by school boards, central offices, state departments of education, and a multitude of national studies. Teachers, I'm sure, find themselves in the position of having to provide it all—along with fulfilling their own goals, if they can.

Our daughter tends to work slowly and carefully and thoughtfully, and gregariously, savoring and wondering about and getting lost in things along the way. Unfortunately, more courses, more homework, more after-school activities, higher expectations, constant time on task, more accountability, and more demands to produce do not represent a very good prescription for her. I believe the word *curriculum* comes from the Latin for "a little race track." Running this race track seven days a week is taking a toll. What does it say that one has to give up membership on the swim team in order to have enough time to get homework done? Even then, why is a sixteen-year-old always the last one to put lights out at night in our house, around midnight? Why is one unable to accompany the family on a weekend in order to get the schoolwork done (or resort to six hours in the back seat of the car with a flashlight)? Where is "time on the margins . . . for reflection, pleasure, and interaction with colleagues?" These are not frills. Humans *learn* through reflection, pleasure, and interaction with colleagues. I do, you do, and high school students do. In short, why do those who move reflectively and precisely and happily either have to abandon reflection, precision, and interaction in order to finish so much so fast—or burn out on the race track? At best, I think we end up with more production and less learning.

As a parent, I accept responsibility to help Joanna comply with more and more demanding work coming at her faster and faster. But I would like to ask the administration and faculty to assume some responsibility as anxiety *reducers* in the school climate for the good of students and for yourselves. Enduring a condition of high anxiety, tension, and pressure for prolonged periods is not good for children, adults, or other living things. How about following the lead of the reputable university downstream and "turn down the throttle setting" a bit?

With appreciation for what all of you are doing and with warm regards,

Sincerely,
Roland

In return I received a cordial, matter-of-fact note from the principal. But my letter probably did not help much to reduce the anxiety level in the school. Indeed, it may even have increased the principal's stress level, which in turn was probably transmitted to others. But it made me feel better. Schoolpeople tend to assume that all parents want more, faster, harder, earlier, for their children. Not all of us do.

I suspect that if they set their mind to it, there are many handles schoolpeople might pull or knobs they might twist that would reduce anxiety while maintaining or even raising standards. We seldom look for these handles, let alone employ them. For instance, when I wrote the letter about my older daughter, my younger daughter was in junior high school. I recall Carolyn being demolished each June by final exams. Tears, sleepless nights, anger, fear, anxiety, all of which could only have reduced learning for her and peace of mind for the rest of us. However, last June she came home relaxed, happy, industrious. She met with classmates and studied into the wee hours of each night without a tear. Curious, I asked her what was going on. "Well, this year," she said, "our team of teachers decided that the final exam scores could only *raise* your year's grade; they couldn't lower it." Simple. The students studied, they cooperated, they remained sane, and I daresay, they learned. I wonder how many other handles and knobs there might be out there?

I would like to be remembered in a school for raising standards and lowering anxiety; I would like to teach in a school with those characteristics. Indeed, I am currently working hard in the classes I teach to achieve this unusual and, for me, critical balance. I am finding that as we approach these conditions, not only does the learning curve rise for students, but both the learning and satisfaction curves rise for me. And I find that a community of learners thrives in the soil of high standards and low anxiety.

Conclusion

That is one conception of a good school. That is the essence of my personal vision. It is not the same as yours, or as anyone else's. Perhaps it does not stress enough basics, or excellence, or equity. Perhaps it is too long-winded. It certainly does not capture the eloquence and beauty of one delightful vision I received from a Minnesota school: "We Care; We Share; We Dare." But it is mine, and a personal vision is, above all, personal. Our visions are part of us. They accompany us wherever we go. Our visions *are* us.

I share my vision here for several reasons: I think it helps pull together and make more coherent many of the ideas outlined in previous sections of this book. It *is* a coat rack that give relatedness to the different pieces. I share my vision because good schools are important to me. Improving schools so they will become good is important to me. I find that a useful vision is generic and has widespread applicability. These characteristics of good schools that I have suggested are not confined to elementary or secondary schools; I feel their realization could transform colleges, universities, and state departments of education, which are equally in need of improvement.

Observers in schools have concluded that the lives of teachers, principals, and students are characterized by brevity, fragmentation, and variety. During an average day, for instance, a teacher or principal engages in several hundred interactions. So do many parents. A personal vision provides a framework with which to react and to make use of the many prescriptions and conceptions of others. But more important, these ideas centered around schools as communities of learners and leaders have provided me with a road map that has enabled me to respond to the hundreds of daily situations in schools and now in a university in a less random and more thoughtful way. Without a vision, I think our behavior becomes reflexive, inconsistent, and shortsighted as we seek the action that will put out the fire fastest so we can get on with putting out the next one. In five years, if we are lucky, our school might be fire free—but it will not have changed much. Anxiety will remain high, humor low, and leadership muddled. Or as one teacher put it in a powerful piece of writing, "Without a clear sense of purpose we get lost, and our activities in school become but empty vessels of our discontent." Seafaring folk put it differently: "For the sailor without a destination, there is no favorable wind."

On the other hand, to the extent that we can look on each hectic school occurrence as an opportunity, to the extent that we can ask of each event, "What is the good news here?" or "How can I make use of this to further my vision?", it may take longer to extinguish the fire. Some may continue to burn. But in five years our school, by successive approximation, will be closer to our vision than it was before. For the sailor *with* a destination, almost every wind can be favorable.

I present my personal vision here to contrast it, and the many similar visions I hear from schoolpeople, with the recent wave of national reports. I find that the personal visions of most school practitioners need no apology. For certain, they differ in important ways from the lists of desirable school qualities constructed by those outside the schools. But these visions of insiders deserve to be taken as seriously as those of outsiders. Not one but two tributaries flow into the knowledge base for improving schools: the social science research literature from the academic community *and* the craft knowledge and vision from the school community. The former is often a mile wide but only an inch deep; the latter is often only an inch wide but a mile deep. Together, they offer remarkable depth and breadth and a fertile meeting place for considering school improvement. Working in a school day after day, or rearing children of their own, entitles schoolpeople and parents to have a vision and to introduce that vision into conversations about school reform.

A final reason I attempt to convey my personal vision here is to suggest that it can be done and to underscore the importance to teachers and parents and principals and students of doing it. The visions of schoolpeople are badly needed in efforts to improve schools. It is not easy. It has not been easy for me, nor do I expect it would be easy for others to distill what they stand for in a few pages.

I wonder how much of our effort in schools is spent trying to help others accept the unacceptable? Too much. Guidance counselors and teachers and social workers and parents expend extraordinary efforts with students toward this end. Principals try to work with teachers so they will accept the unacceptable. And how much energy, on the other hand, do we spend trying to change the unacceptable? Not enough. We can do more to replace the unacceptable with the acceptable if we clarify our vision of a preferred school world, reveal it in neon lights, and draw upon it as a compass to guide our work. Many advocates of the effective schools movement have observed that when a school becomes effective, it still has to become good. I wonder whether it is possible to start with a good school. Once a school is good, I suspect that it will also be effective.

I do not believe that a teacher or principal or professor can be a serious agent of change within a school, operating only from someone else's prescription or vision. Implementing the ideas and ideals of others will always be a halfhearted enterprise. To be sure, finding ways to comply with the needs and goals of the larger organization is important to the survival of the organization and to each of us who is a part of it. But developing ways to foster the elements of teachers' and principals' personal visions is a full-hearted, badly needed form of school improvement.

Zen Buddhism advises us that "to train a bull it is sometimes necessary to enlarge the fences." We might add that to improve a school it is sometimes necessary to enlarge those four walls that surround the future. Expansion of vision within the schoolhouse is an enterprise that will bring about the kinds of schools in which there is room for all of us to live and work and have our children learn. When we create schools we value for our children and ourselves, we will have created schools of value to others as well.

References

Adler, M. J. *The Paideia Proposal: An Educational Manifesto.* New York: Macmillan, 1982.

Barth, R. S. *Run School Run.* Cambridge, Mass.: Harvard University Press, 1980.

Barth, R. S. "The Principal as Staff Developer." *Boston University Journal of Education,* 1981a, *163* (2), 144–163.

Barth, R. S. "A Principal's Center." *Journal of Staff Development,* 1981b, *2* (1), 53–69.

Barth, R. S. "Now What?" *Principal,* 1982a, *61* (4), 8–9.

Barth, R. S. "Public Education and the Secular Ministry: Educators Possess the Power to Restore Themselves." *Education Week,* 1982b, *2* (7), 15, 20.

Barth, R. S. "Writing About Practice." In T. M. Amabile and M. L. Stubbs (eds.), *Psychological Research in the Classroom: Issues for Educators and Researchers.* Elmsford, N.Y.: Pergamon Press, 1982c.

Barth, R. S. "Can We Make a Match of Schools and Universities?" *Education Week,* 1984a, *4* (13), 16, 24.

Barth, R. S. "Must Colleagues Become Adversaries?" *Principal,* 1984b, *63* (5), 52–53.

Barth, R. S. "The Professional Development of Principals." *Educational Leadership,* 1984c, *42* (2), 93–94.

Barth, R. S. "Sandboxes and Honeybees." *Education Week,* 1984d, *3* (33), 24.

Barth, R. S. "The Leader as Learner." *Educational Leadership,* 1985a, *42* (6), 92–93.

Barth, R. S. "Outside Looking In—Inside Looking In." *Phi Delta Kappan,* 1985b, *66* (5), 356–358.

181

Barth, R. S. "The Principal and the Profession of Teaching." *Elementary School Journal,* 1986a, *86* (4), 471–492.

Barth, R. S. "Principal Centered Professional Development." *Theory into Practice,* 1986b, *25* (3), 156–160.

Barth, R. S. "On Sheep and Goats and School Reform." *Phi Delta Kappan,* 1986c, *68* (4), 293–296.

Barth, R. S. "School as a Community of Leaders." In A. Lieberman (ed.), *Building a Professional Culture in Schools.* New York: Teachers College Press, 1988.

Blumberg, A., and Greenfield, W. *The Effective Principal.* Boston: Allyn and Bacon, 1980.

Boyer, E. L. *High School: A Report on Secondary Education in America.* New York: Harper & Row, 1983.

Carnegie Forum on Education and the Economy. *A Nation Prepared: Teachers for the 21st Century.* Washington, D.C.: Carnegie Forum on Education and the Economy, 1986.

Center for Policy Research and Analysis, National Governors' Association. *Time for Results: The Governors' 1991 Report on Education.* Washington, D.C.: National Governors' Association, 1986.

Edmonds, R. "Effective Schools for the Urban Poor." *Educational Leadership,* 1979, *37* (1), 15–24.

Elam, S. M. "The Second Gallup/Phi Delta Kappan Poll of Teachers' Attitudes Toward the Public Schools." *Phi Delta Kappan,* 1989, *70* (10), 785–798.

Goodlad, J. I. *A Place Called School.* New York: McGraw-Hill, 1984.

Graves, D. "Research Update: A New Look in Writing Research." *Language Arts,* 1980, *57* (8), 913–918.

Holmes Group. *Tomorrow's Teachers: A Report of the Holmes Group.* Holmes Group, 1986.

Levine, S., Barth, R. S., and Haskins, K. "The Harvard Principals' Center: School Leaders as Adult Learners." In J. Murphy and P. Hallinger (eds.), *Approaches to Administrative Training in Education.* Albany, N.Y.: State University of New York Press, 1987.

Lipsitz, J. *Successful Schools for Young Adolescents.* New Brunswick, N.J.: Transaction Books, 1984.

Little, J. W. *School Success and Staff Development in Urban*

Desegregated Schools: A Summary of Recently Completed Research. Boulder, Colo.: Center for Action Research, April 1981.

Lortie, D. C. *Schoolteacher: A Sociological Study.* Chicago: University of Chicago Press, 1975.

National Commission on Excellence in Education. *A Nation at Risk: The Imperative for Educational Reform.* Washington, D.C.: National Commission on Excellence in Education, 1983.

Principals' Center Spring Calendar. Cambridge, Mass.: Graduate School of Education, Harvard University, January 1987.

Rodman, B. "Administrators' Group Outlines Positions." *Education Week,* 1987, *6* (22), 9.

Rutter, M., Maughan, B., Mortimore, P., and Ouston, J. *Fifteen Thousand Hours: Secondary Schools and Their Effects on Children.* Cambridge, Mass.: Harvard University Press, 1979.

Sarason, S. B. *The Culture of the School and the Problem of Change.* (2nd ed.) Boston: Allyn and Bacon, 1982.

Sizer, T. R. *Horace's Compromise: The Dilemma of the American High School.* Boston: Houghton Mifflin, 1984.

Stomberg, R. D. "The Goose." Unpublished poem, 1982.

Ventures in Good Schooling. Washington, D.C.: National Education Association and National Association of Secondary School Principals, 1986.

Index